Contemporary Christian Social Concerns Series

General Editor: E. P. Smith

Volume One

Unemployment Under The Judgement Of God
by Peter Mayhew

By the same author:
JUSTICE IN INDUSTRY (S.C.M. 1980)

UNEMPLOYMENT UNDER THE JUDGEMENT OF GOD

UNEMPLOYMENT UNDER THE JUDGEMENT OF GOD

by
PETER MAYHEW

CHURCHMAN PUBLISHING LIMITED
WORTHING: 1985

Unemployment Under The Judgement Of God
was first published by

Churchman Publishing Limited
117 Broomfield Avenue
Worthing
West Sussex BN14 7SF

in 1985

© Copyright Peter Mayhew

ISBN 1 85093 025 2
All Rights Reserved

Distributed to the book trade by

Bailey Bros. & Swinfen Limited
Warner House
Folkestone
Kent CT19 6PH

Churchman's Agents in Canada

Jonathan Gould Books of Winnipeg

Made and Printed in Great Britain by

Whitstable Litho Limited
Whitstable
Kent CT5 3PP

To
Bishop David Jenkins and Canon John Atherton
of The William Temple Foundation
In Gratitude

Contents

Unemployment Under The Judgement Of God

Preface

British unemployment in 1985 reached the highest figure ever. That is tragedy. This book is primarily about unemployment. It is about the un-naturalness of absence of work for the human being, about the immorality of tolerating mass unemployment, about the need to make its abolition a national priority. There will, of course, always be some unemployed who are 'in between' jobs; and there will always be, alas, some unemployables. However, both these categories constitute small minorities of the unemployed.

Because the book is about unemployment, it has also necessarily to be about work. It is the absence of work which basically constitutes unemployment; it is the importance of work for human beings which makes unemployment serious for them and for society as a whole. I shall try in the first chapter to explain what I mean by work and why I think it to be dehumanizing to be without it. Then I shall illustrate my thesis with an account of the experiences of various workers.

I shall go on in the third chapter to explain that I do not hold or advocate the so-called Protestant Work Ethic, at least in the sense in which it was propagated in the 17, 18, and 19th centuries. In the fourth chapter, I shall defend the ancient Greeks from the common idea that they despised work. I shall also try to show that various categories of persons who appear to lead a happy, carefree life, without doing any honest work, are in fact not so happy as we, in our ignorance, may suppose. They do not in fact fulfil their true selves or gain satisfaction from doing nothing, even when they are financially provided for.

I am defending and attempting to propagate a doctrine of man as by nature a worker. I believe that behind nature there is God who made man to be a worker. I attempt in Chapter 5 to enunciate a theology of this, both one 'from above', based on biblical revelation, and one 'from below', a grass roots theology. If the reader seeking judgement upon unemployment grows impatient as I discuss work, let him bear in mind that I am trying to build up an altogether devastating case against the toleration of unemployment, by proving that man needs work in order to be man. So, at last, I come in Chapters 6, 7, and 8, to consider the awful facts of unemployment, especially of the unemployment of the young. I begin to suggest how we can (and ought to) deal with it.

In Chapter 9, I try to show how and why some work is in fact unhappy work, and to suggest how education and training might not only make that kind of work more satisfying but how they might also help to produce a worker more concerned with his workless brother (and sister). Finally, in Chapter 10, I suggest that it is unlikely that mass unemployment in Britain will be cured without sacrifice from many members of the community. This may well involve work-sharing, with shorter hours of work and with reduction of income for some. I go on to declare that, for Christians at least, the vision which may inspire them most will be that of the kingdom of God, into which they will seek to enter more fully by the resolute doing of God's will for his poor unemployed and for his working people too.

1

The Human Need to Work

The miners' dispute of 1984-5 was not a revolutionary attempt to gain political power. The mining communities already in 1984 had long term unemployment running at about 20%. It was a desperate effort by a collection of threatened mining communities to prevent further loss of jobs owing to mine closures. Whole communities gave up their main source of income temporarily for fear lest the miners lose their jobs for ever. Only those who know the miners can appreciate how true all this is. Only those who know the fear of unemployment can understand it.

I crossed a churchyard recently and stumbled clumsily over a large young bird on the footpath. I picked him up and found him, to my relief, undamaged. I should have been on my guard, for the cawing of two older birds overhead had been going on before I came across the young one. I looked up and saw them as they flew over the churchyard again and again. I supposed that they were warning me off. However, when I approached the churchyard again a couple of hours later, they were still flying and cawing, and had obviously been doing so all morning. This, in fact, went on, apparently ceaselessly, for several days. I came to understand that it was not a show to frighten off clumsy strangers like myself but was designed to encourage the young bird to get off his feet, to use his wings, and to take to the air, his natural milieu. It was intolerable to the older birds that the young one should maintain his quite unnatural bird-life on the ground. They were determined by ceaseless effort to encourage him to fly, to get him into the air. This eventually, presumably happened.

I am going to try to show in this book that work is as natural (and as necessary) for human beings as flying is for birds. Where there is no work, there is danger of dehumanization. I am going to plead that those who are in work ought to do all in their power to make it possible for those out of work to obtain it. I am going to ask them to strive and struggle and sacrifice in the cause of the unemployed.

In this first chapter I shall try to explain what I mean by that 'work' which I consider to be vitally needful for man. The word 'work' means different things to different people. Let me make it as plain here as I possibly can that by work I do not mean paid employment. By work I mean any kind of purposeful activity mental or physical which is (or is intended to be) of beneficent social significance. Later in this chapter I shall quote the psychologist who says that the work which satisfies is work which alters the environment. The cleaner of the toilets may (and in fact, to my knowledge, sometimes does) get vast satisfaction from the doing of a job which is creative in the sense that it does alter the environment and is of obvious beneficent social significance. He receives little, if any, commendation from his 'customers', gains no public approbation, enjoys perhaps the very opposite of prestige. Yet he may be a proud and satisfied man. 'You are the most important person in this place,' the convener at Chloride Batteries, Swinton, used to say to his toilet cleaner. Not all would need such high praise to gain satisfaction. 'Spam' Blakeman is a worker. He is a pensioner and a widower. He sweeps away all day in my friend's barber shop. He looks after his aged mother and cooks her dinner for her. He works hard, is a satisfied man. He is available for jobs and errands of all kinds. I must make it plain that the purposeful, environment-changing activity, which is to satisfy and which is to be worthy of the name 'work', must be of a demanding kind. The housewife who daintily dusts when she knows that she ought to scrub gains no great satisfaction from her activity. The man who 'potters' in his garden when hard weeding is required will only gain satisfaction if old age or infirmity render him incapable of doing more. The full-time gardener, toiling at his back-bending work, will gain great satisfaction, even if he is on a pension and is not paid for it. Indeed, I repeat that, in stressing the need and demanding the right for all to work, in pleading for the nation to accept the ending of mass unemployment as national necessity, I do not mean to sound as if I am saying that all satisfying work needs to be paid work. Sources of income other than wages and salaries are sometimes available: profits, for example, and inherited income. My friend, the late Maurice Reckitt of the Christendom Group, only did one paid job (for two years) during the whole of his long life. However, he worked hard all that life, organizing, writing, speaking. His purposeful activity in some measure altered the thinking of the Church through his influence upon Archbishop

William Temple (as illustrated in the Malvern Conference of 1941). What I am saying most emphatically is that a mere leisure activity, a hobby, a game played as an amateur, is no substitute for that purposeful activity which normally alters the environment and which is what I mean by work, whether it be paid or unpaid.

I must add here (and I shall develop the theme more fully in chapter 9) that for work to be satisfying, to be truly 'humanizing' to a person, it needs to be undertaken in decent, humane conditions. It is best, in fact, when it is undertaken in community, where there is genuine fellowship, true co-operation with others. This uses and develops the 'herd instinct', the human need to be associated with others. All this adds up towards that full humanization in which men realize themselves and also help to realize society.

If I have not yet made plain what I mean by that work which human beings need, which the deprived unemployed need, I shall try later in this chapter and throughout this book to make that meaning more clear. Very shortly, I shall try to show by quoting some psychologists why I believe that what I call work fulfils human personality, humanizes. But here, first of all, in my attempt to convince the reader of the need to work which almost all persons have, let me give a few examples of persons who continue to struggle to do some honest work, despite obstacles such as old age and debility. This noble struggle goes on not because they want to gain personal or popular approbation, but because they need to be themselves, to fulfil, to realize themselves.

First of all, I call to witness a lady of more than 90, a resident in an old persons' home. Her eyes and her legs are weak. She is stitching away by her bedside at a cushion-cover of many colours. She says that she is 'showing off in a nice way'. She tells me that she means to go on at this sort of work 'so long as there is any breath left in my body'. She is determined in so doing to be herself. In fact without that stitching she would be less than herself. Almost immediately after I had written these lines, an elderly person in a state of acute depression said to me, 'If only I could do my work, I would be all right'. Yesterday, a woman wrote to me, 'Work is a healthy thing. . . . God help me if my gifts are taken from me'. I knew just what she meant. We shall consider some of the problems of the aged and the retired in the next chapter. It is the theme of this book that no one should have nothing to do unless he or she is incapable of doing anything.

I recall vividly a group discussing 'my' theory of work and humanization in a flat in a Midland city. There were two youngish priests there. One was concerned intimately with problems of industry and one with unemployment. There was a man there who, although temporarily employed, had recently been for a long time out of work. His unemployed state was likely to be resumed very shortly. There were also in the room two competent and dedicated managers. None of those present were particularly impressed by my belief in work as an important element in humanization. However, as the conversation warmed up, inhibitions seemed to wear off and significant things were said. People spoke as they felt, and their feeling seemed to me to be realistic. 'When a man is unemployed,' said a priest, 'he goes to ground.' The unemployed, he added, coped by withdrawing. 'It's like emasculation,' he said, 'it's "de-manning".' The man in a temporary state of suspension from unemployment said quietly that he had had fifty-three weeks of unemployment. He said that the first few weeks were all right. He could do what he wanted to do when he wanted to do it. Then suddenly, he said, he found himself in the first of a series of bouts of depression. He became short of money. He could not, as he said, compete with his peer group. He could not smoke with them, drink with them as before. He worked out a routine for his daily visits to the city's various job centres, learned what to look for at each and when to look for it. Each tended to specialize in different jobs. Then came a much deeper, much longer depression, an almost suicidal one, 'despair' as he called it. Now he was doing an Open University course. He was getting substantial grants for it. He said if it was not for that he would 'go quite useless'. Unemployment, he said, was debilitating. One of the priests said that men worked primarily for money. The former unemployed man disagreed. He said that 'what matters is having something to do'. It was an illuminating evening, very real.

We are considering human beings and their needs. So we turn to psychology, the science of the mind. I am claiming that work (which may often contribute to physical fitness) will, if it is the right kind of work, done in the right conditions, contribute to the well-being of the human mind as well, will contribute to full humanization. There is a regrettable lack of a psychology of work amongst modern psychologists. I myself studied psychology at Oxford under the Wylde Reader, the late Dr William Brown (1881-1952). He caused us to read the works of Professor William McDougall. The portrait of the one and the bust of the other are to be seen in the Department of Psychology building at Oxford. From McDougall I learned to look out for 'an instinct of construction' in man. He declared that the 'constructive play of young children, their delight in making things, especially houses, caves and shelters, are perhaps the most direct evidences of the presence of this instinct in man'.[1] Earlier, McDougall had written: 'We seem to be justified in assuming in man an instinct of construction. The playful activities of children seem to be in part determined by its impulse . . . The simple desire to make something, rooted in this instinct, is probably a contributing motive to all human constructions, from a mud-pie to a metaphysical system or a code of laws.'[2] What McDougall wrote perhaps scarcely covers all sorts of work. I am thinking of that kind of apparently 'un-creative' work which people sometimes rashly describe as 'soul-destroying'. I shall deal with this later. Nor would most modern psychologists go along confidently with McDougall and his 'instinct of construction'. However, psychologists in the University and at the Oxford Polytechnic assure me that there is still respect for the name and word of William McDougall.

We must turn towards writers of a later generation. Frank Bechhofer, Jennifer Platt, John Goldthorpe and David Lockwood, all sociologists financed by the Cambridge Department of Applied Economics, published in 1968 *The Affluent Worker*. In it they say that 'ego-involvement in work is strong'. They go on to say of work that it 'represents a central life interest in that, in addition to its instrumental significance, it is also of some major importance in satisfying workers' expressive and affective needs'.[3] F. Herzberg wrote in the same year, quoting Jung, Adler, Sullivan, Rogers, Goldstein, Maslow and Gardner as his authorities, that 'the supreme goal of man is to fulfil himself, as a creative, unique individual, according to his own innate possibilities'.[4] A young gardener, a graduate in philosophy of a Scottish university, assured me that for work to be satisfying to him pay is not strictly necessary (although he himself certainly needs it for the support of his wife and children). He says that what he needs far more than the pay is the sense of being of some sort of use, of fulfilling some sort of function. He says that he would not get such a sense from gardening (or painting) merely for himself; whereas he says that he would get it if he were fulfilling some sort of voluntary social service, even if it were unpaid. So he worked happily away at gardening for an Oxford community of nuns, but is unlikely ever to become a rich man.

Dr Michael Argyle, of the Oxford University Department of Experimental Psychology, stands by his 1972 statement that 'workers as well as managers work partly because of the intrinsic satisfaction derived from working'. 'Possibly', he wrote then, 'sheer activity is rewarding.'[5] He recalls experiments which show that rats like running in activity wheels and exploring mazes, while monkeys enjoy solving puzzles and manipulating equipment. An able young lecturer in psychology at the Oxford Polytechnic admitted to me (when pressed) that 'there may be in man a latent need to produce, to create'. The admission was a little grudging. Yet person after person has recalled to me the saying of Freud that the basic requirements of human existence are 'to love and to work'.[6] It would have greatly simplified my task if Freud had enlarged upon this theme. I asked a young truck-driver if he enjoyed his work. He replied that 'you have to enjoy it'. He seemed to mean that there is something in you that makes you enjoy it (although you may sometimes pretend the very opposite).

We shall try to see in chapter 9 why some workers do not enjoy their work. However, now let us look hard at the very important writing of Ives Hendrick. W. S. Neff draws our attention to this Harvard psycho-analyst and to the significance of his few but authoritative publications.[7] Messrs John Hayes and Peter Nutman of the Tavistock Clinic, writing in 1981, also quote Dr Hendrick.[8] The importance of his 1943 writings seems to me to be very considerable. Hendrick himself describes his 'theory of an instinct to master'.[9] He writes of 'one of the ego instincts',[10] 'whose goal is control or alteration of environmental situations through the effective development of integrated intellectual and motor functions'.[11] Work, he says, is motivated 'by the need for

6

the efficient use of the central nervous system for the performance of the well-integrated ego functions which enable the individual to control or alter his environment'[12]. His work theory is of the human need to control or alter the environment. He himself cites Doctors Thomas French, Karl Menninger and Robert Welder as protagonists of this theory.[13] John Hayes and Peter Nutman sum up his theory by writing that pleasure in work is a consequence of the gratification of the instinct to master or alter the environment. Hendrick himself had written that 'the work principle is a satisfaction of an instinct by well-organized activity'.[14] He said that he himself would have preferred to call this 'instinct to master' simply 'the ego instinct', but that Freud had used that term so freely that he chose to use one more capable of exact definition.[15] He re-defined it as 'the drive impelling to integration and skilful performance, and therefore the incentive to the development and exercise of the ego functions, which are mentally and emotionally experienced as the need to perform work efficiently'.[16] I may, I hope, be allowed to shorten this account of the urge towards work in man and to define it in some at least of Hendrick's words as 'the drive . . . to perform work efficiently'. Hendrick himself sums up in all humility by writing that his 'discourse is, after all, only a fancy version of common sense'.[17] It is a very carefully and compellingly formulated version of common sense.

It is interesting to see Hendrick's urge for 'the individual to control or alter his environment' in all sorts of work which are not normally regarded as 'creative'. He himself draws attention to the housewife who is taking 'pleasure in cleaning up'. As a good Freudian, he apologizes for finding no certain sign of sexual gratification in this process. In fact, he says, she is simply 'performing work', and in those hours of housework obtaining pleasure from a 'job well done, in efficient performance of a useful task'.[18] My own mother, in an old age less sheltered than her gilded youth, gained enormous satisfaction by a quite unnecessary daily domestic spring cleaning. My young Australian friend of a literary bent, when obliged to take to her bed for a long period before her confinement, at first looked forward to abundant time for reading. Before long she found herself longing for knitting or cleaning or any other kind of work. My English friend, a former nursing sister, now the mother of several grown up children, finds herself at 50 mentally devastated for lack of work. Young Australian and middle-aged Englishwoman seek with heart and soul for something to do 'to master or alter the environment'. In each of them there is the inward 'drive to perform work efficiently'.

I believe Hendrick to be unanswerable. The urge, the drive is there, at least in all who have had a normal background. Alvin Gouldner in the concluding essay of *Work 2: 20 Personal Accounts*, writes of work as 'therefore one of the principal ways in which we make ourselves'.[19] If anyone doubts this, let him go to the Oxford Industrial Training Unit for the handicapped (for subnormal adults). There he will see more than a hundred handicapped persons working happily at their benches day by day from 9am to 4pm, making objects of commercial value ordered by local firms. They even turn out specialized products needed only in small numbers. The supply of work to them is maintained because of the quality of their work. The contract work is constructive, writes their manager, and demands discipline and care. The correct labels must go on the boxes, the components must be assembled perfectly. Skills such as sewing and cutting are acquired slowly, and there is training in the use of machinery. Some of the trainees learn to help one another. 'We have found that the older subnormals tend to look after the severely subnormal. They mother and father them.' At different rates they grow in capacity, develop humanly. They had had difficulties at school, had grown up in dread of being of no use, of having nothing to do, of unemployment. Now they make goods that are needed for British Leyland just up the road. The goods they make are of considerable value and are paid for at commercial rates. The dignity of the handicapped person is restored and protected, his cheerful satisfaction in his work shines out of him. It is difficult to speak of what one sees amongst employed handicapped persons without running the risk of being accused of exaggeration or sentimentality. There the drive to perform work efficiently is being fully used, there the environment is being altered, there the handicapped are finding themselves at least partially fulfilled. The satisfaction of the handicapped workers in their work leads to high productivity.

For the unemployed, handicapped or unhandicapped, there is no productivity, no satisfaction. Professor Chris Freeman, head of the Science Policy Research Unit of Sussex University, writes:

> I share the view of Marie Jahoda, Freud and Marx . . .: the psychological
> as well as the economic consequences of unemployment can be devastating
> for individuals and societies, because work, both formal and informal, is
> the means by which people in most different cultures relate to each other
> and to the world, and acquire a sense of dignity and purpose, even though
> many jobs are boring and hard.[20]

When engines from Cummins Engineering (of Daventry) go out
to different parts of the world there are metal tags upon them with
the names of the workers who assembled them and of those who
inspected them. There is pride, and there is responsibility, and
there is interest in Daventry and in Africa as they become
personally linked. The fact that the metal tags are sometimes used
as parts of necklaces for African ladies makes the link no less real.

Professor Freeman suggests that the boring and hard may still
have dignity and purpose. A worker on a production line, let it be
said (and he will say it for himself), may be well satisfied with his
job. An intelligent middle-aged woman said to me: 'I don't want
to be creative. I just want to be employed.' Work does in fact
confer upon the worker some sort of status; it gives him an
identity. 'It is identity which matters,' said a friend of mine with
great emphasis. It is not so much what others think of the worker
but rather what he thinks of himself. 'I'm a window-cleaner,' the
young man says to me, to explain why he is working so hard. That
seems to him to be a reasonable explanation. No more needs to be
said.

With the unemployed, it is different. Francesca Inskipp, at a
Liverpool conference in 1981, declared that it is difficult for the
unemployed person to find his identity, because part of one's
identity is to be found in one's job. The son of a friend has
recently committed suicide because of persistent failure to secure
a job. He felt no desire to continue to exist without one. A priest
told me at the end of a long period out of work, that he was in fact
'dead' (although physically alive). Wolfhart Pannenberg wrote of
man's need for 'openness to the world', for being 'related to the
world', to counteract his self-centredness.[21] Work gives man such
a relationship. Work helps as well, as we know, to confer status,
to give identity. That is true. Yet I maintain that, above all, it
satisfies the need for purposeful activity, of mind and of body too.

I am Ives Hendrick's man; I accept and wish to promote his teaching that the drive to perform work efficiently, to master, to alter the environment, is part of the make-up of man, that its satisfaction is necessary normally to his humanization. We can say that work is the fulfilment of purposeful activity of social significance. To be fulfilling to me it must be for some social end. Ives Hendrick's definition breaks down slightly, when the vandal satisfies his urge to alter the environment by smashing and burning. Two burglar friends of mine recently sat in my living room discussing different 'jobs' they had done. Burglary was their 'work', and by it they certainly altered the environment. So perhaps Ives Hendrick's definition of work must give way to that above: purposeful activity of social significance.

Some form of creativity is vital for a person, even if it be the sweeping of a road or washing up in a hotel kitchen. A friend of mine, recently returned to his invariable state of unemployment from the briefest of stays in prison (his first experience of it), gives me in great simplicity and sincerity his impressions. He was, he said, surprised and delighted to discover that there was work to do in prison (even a little money to be earned). Who would have thought it? Nicolas Berdyaev wrote that 'man is more eager than ever to create,' that 'the ethics of creativeness spring from personality'. He declared: 'Creativeness and a creative attitude to life as a whole is not man's right, it is his duty. It is a moral imperative that applies in every department of life.'[22] Of the right to fulfil this duty, to obey this moral imperative, the unemployed person is deprived. Humanly speaking, unemployment is disastrous. To be unemployed is to be maimed. Mass unemployment is mass dehumanization. In a letter to *The Times* of 28 January 1983, the Bishop of Lincoln pleaded for a Christian contribution to politics, for the serious putting forward of the case for ensuring that the individual be permitted to find the meaning of himself in society, to 'relate himself to others', so that he may be 'fulfilled in community'.[23]

NOTES

1 *An Outline of Psychology*, Methuen, 1969, p. 162 (1st published 1923).
2 *Introduction to Social Psychology*, Methuen, 1980, p. 75 (1st published 1908).
3 Cambridge University Press, p. 41.
4 *Work and the Nature of Man*, Staples Press, p. 56.
5 *The Social Psychology of Work*, Penguin, 1974, p. 9 (1st published 1972).
6 W. S. Neff: *Work and Human Behavior*, Atherton Press, New York, 1960, p. 4.
7 *Work and Human Behavior (op. cit.)*, p. 91.
8 *Understanding the Unemployed*, Tavistock Publications, 1981, p. 41.
9 *Psycho-analytic Quarterly*, 1943, B. p. 561.
10 ibid., p. 564.
11 *Psycho-analytic Quarterly*, 1943, A. p. 311.
12 ibid., p. 315.
13 ibid., p. 311.
14 ibid., p. 316.
15 *Psycho-analytic Quarterly*, 1943, B. p. 564.
16 *Psycho-analytic Quarterly*, 1943, A. p. 314.
17 ibid., p. 328.
18 ibid., p. 323.
19 Penguin 1969, p. 7.
20 *The Microelectronics Revolution*, Basil Blackwell, 1980, p. 311.
21 *What is Man?* Fortress Press, Philadelphia, 1977, p. 81 (1st published 1962).
22 *The Destiny of Man*, Geoffrey Bles, 1937, pp. 22, 169.
23 p. 13.

2

The Worker

I am desperately striving to make the reader of this book fully aware of the chronic and urgent need of the unemployed to find work. I am assuming that the reader is himself (or herself) likely to be at work. People at work sometimes read. The unemployed read very little. They can read all day if they like (and all night). In fact even the intellectuals amongst them find that they cannot read much. They just lose their taste for reading, with unlimited opportunity for it. That is one of the things that unemployment does to a person.

My task is made difficult for me by the fact that there is a convention that work is 'a dirty word', a popular tradition according to which work is 'a bad thing'. People simply do not mean what they say when they talk like that. My friend, Paul Rathkey, Head of Research at the Jim Conway Foundation (of Stockton), writes in a report for the Foundation: 'It is wrong to assume that work is of central importance, or even of major importance, to the life interests of every individual.'[1] I believe him to be entirely mistaken and shall do my utmost to prove him so. The unemployed know very well that work is of importance to a person's life.

Studs Terkel, in his *Working*, describes work as 'violence to the spirit as well as to the body . . . daily humiliation'.[2] In Ronald Fraser's *Work (Twenty Personal Accounts)*, his unemployed man who reads *The Scotsman* and *The Guardian* in the Miners' Institute (and James Boswell before going to bed at night) declares: 'Frankly, I hate work.'[3] There are many at work who have not suffered unemployment and who feel that it would be wonderful not to have to get up at 6am on five days of the week, to have an utterly relaxed day until one summons up enough energy to do a little gardening in one's own time. The unemployed know all too well that unemployment does not work out like that. The unemployed reader in the Miners' Institute is no fool. He goes on immediately to add that in fact he loves work, that it is supremely interesting, often fascinating. In other words, it is true of him, as of many another, that he does not really hate work as much as he says that he does.

There has been a good deal of research into attitudes to work. Before I consider the validity of this, I want to give an account of a visit to the Daimler Limousine Assembly Plant which seemed to confirm that workers' real opinion of their work is not to be judged by what they say about it. I visited (twice) Jaguar Cars at Browns Lane, Allesley, Coventry. When I first entered the Daimler Limousine Assembly Plant there, I was immediately introduced to a small group of managers and foremen. When it was explained that I was someone who was researching into work, there were the conventional derogatory remarks, made with smiles, concerning that unsavoury subject. I went through the plant slowly, watching men working in small teams, some of them in teams of only two persons. I saw a foreman sitting on the floor doing (and demonstrating) a job, watched with fascination by a team of five or six fellow-workers. It was emphasized to me that in the Assembly Plant the aim was to have every man capable of doing every job, every man able to assemble a Daimler by himself. The supervision seemed to me to be sensitive, the self-motivation amongst the workers outstanding. All concerned understood that they were doing quality work, and all seemed to be proud of it. There was a minimum absenteeism rate (of .01%). The young manager said to me quietly that he believed British engineering to be the best in the world. As I prepared to leave, the foreman who had taken charge of me and who had been among the group who had originally sneered at the mention of work as a subject for research, cleared his throat. There was obviously something which he was anxious to say before I left the plant. He said (to my amazement), 'I must say that it's a joy to work here'. That was strong language. The comment had not been solicited. Earlier in the morning, a worker had said to me, 'I've been here for twenty-three years, and I'm proud to be associated with Jaguar'.

During my other visit, I was in the Jaguar Assembly Plant with its assembly line three-quarters of a mile long. Women at their sewing machines working on the fault-free imported Scandinavian leather seemed to me to be working too hard (but quite cheerfully). Men were working on what they proudly called 'the finest engine in the world'. We shall see later, in dealing with happiness (and unhappiness) at work, how important it is, whenever possible, to secure from hourly paid workers a willing

14

concentration on quality. Throughout Jaguar Cars there was minute inspection to eliminate the slightest visible imperfection. Faults were remedied along the line or at a rectification area at the end of the line. Each car had its own number (for checking purposes), as every Jaguar car has had its own number since 1928. In pursuit of near-perfection every worker seemed in some measure involved. The hides from Scandinavia (where there are no barbed wire fences to tear the skins) are cut by hand and sewn like fine tailoring, with two hides sewn together for the seats in each vehicle. One sees the walnut veneers on a backing of mahogany being cut for the dashboards so that the pattern on each side shall exactly match. A suggestion scheme was prominently advertised. All under management level could win up to £2000 (tax free) for suggestions for improvements in production methods, in economies in use of materials, in reduction of maintenance costs and in safety precautions. A list of recent winners (and their substantial financial rewards) was on the board. 'It's skill that keeps Jaguar going,' someone said to me. There seemed to be a quiet satisfaction and a sense of pride throughout that place. Management offices were near the shop floor, managers in and out of them onto the floor. A worker said that it gave him confidence that the managing director had chosen to live near his place of work. 'And he's married to a Leamington girl,' he added. Another remarked that 'you have to work where your heart is'. His heart was with Jaguar Cars.

Personal research suggesting that work is satisfying to man may well be more valid than that research which comes to contrary conclusions and which is based on written replies to questionnaires. In both cases, it is difficult to exclude the presuppositions with which one begins from the conclusions to which one comes. Sometimes the form in which the questions are put reflects the answers which one hopes to obtain. This might be more true of American than British industrial research. At any rate, written questionnaires do sometimes produce strange results, sometimes results which are unreliable. People are sometimes frivolous in their written answers to questions which they may feel to be stupid or impertinent. Many do not care to 'give themselves away' on paper. Sometimes there is suspicion, sometimes a getting together of those concerned to give agreed answers. To some the questionnaire is just one unnecessary paper to be thoughtlessly and hastily filled in. It is sometimes answered in very great haste. The results vary in value.

Dr Michael Argyle pointed out to me that researchers by no means always relied solely upon written questionnaires. For example, in *The Affluent Worker: Industrial Attitudes and Behaviour*, J. H. Goldthorpe, D. Lockwood, F. Bechhofer and J. Platt write that their team interviewed 250 persons at their place of work and 229 of these, with their wives, in their own homes.[4] One is nevertheless obliged to ask to what extent they managed to gain the confidence of those interviewed and to what extent they gained honest answers to their questioning. On the other hand, the authors of *Living with Capitalism*[5] were members of a team of Bristol University sociologists who spent three years almost daily in and out of a West Country chemical plant, interviewing 118 workers (and their managers) at their place of work. They talked to some of them also in their homes and over drinks in public houses. With management sanction they would sometimes spend several hours at a time with one worker. They established relationships; and my personal knowledge of both authors and of their methods confirms my belief in the extraordinary value of their evidence. However, even with such painstaking and carefully recorded evidence, one has to be careful lest bias cause over-weighting of one kind of evidence and the omission or minimizing of other sorts.

It is difficult to estimate one's own impartiality or one's own prejudices. I can only say with sincerity that I entered into my current research with an open (and indeed an ignorant) mind and was constantly surprised by what I found. I was careful, so far as possible, to put no answers into persons' mouths. Most people seem to me to have been frank and honest with me. The researcher ought to report what he does not like and what does not conform to his ideas as objectively as he reports what supports him. Even a writer like Terkel (who claims to abhor work) reports his two American newsboys. 'I like my work,' says one, 'it's fun throwing papers.' The other one testifies: 'It's good to be a newsboy.'[6] Here are two lads quietly (or not so quietly) expressing their satisfaction with their work, their purposeful evening activity of social significance (as they change the environment of the American city where the arrival of the evening paper still constitutes one of the events of the day). I saw the thing happening as a child in the little Kentucky town where I grew up, and I watched with fascination its continuing happening in a recent summer in the same town now double its size. Studs Terkel quite mistakenly dismisses the testimony of the newboys as that of 'the happy few who find a savor in their daily job'.[7] My mind switches over to the Welsh lads in Rhonnda Enterprise, Porth, whom I shall describe later in this chapter and to others in the Rhonnda Valley, hopeful, cheerful, as they looked forward to or in fact already enjoyed their work. All this I have seen against the ghastly background of Welsh unemployment.

Now let me say something about Netherton Farm. Near Ross-on-Wye, as one reaches it from Gloucester, there is a typical farm gate leading (one imagines) to a typical farm. It is a dairy farm, inherited by Paul Scudamore. In addition to the farm, there are also located there Farmplan Computers and Farmplan Cow Kennels. Farmplan Computers encourage farmers all over the United Kingdom (and beyond) to use computers as an aid to competent farming. Computers report on individual cows or on groups of cows, on milkers, for example, deviating from norm. They work out cropping programmes, formulate ration systems, calculate volumes and storage space. Farmplan Cow Kennels provide buildings for farm animals. These are designed to be roomy, well-ventilated, durable. Around Paul Scudamore's office in one of the old farm buildings, people seem to be always on the run. They run up and down the stairs, smiling as they go. I asked myself why they all seemed to run. They are exceptionally busy, mostly working in two large upstairs rooms, working close to one another, seemingly deriving job satisfaction in particular from their team work. The word 'team' seems to be used frequently at Netherton. Paul Scudamore believes that hard work in co-operation is natural to man. Certainly the smiles of the youngish men and women running up and down the stairs seemed natural enough. I was permitted to speak personally to whom I wished for as long as I wished. The pressure appeared to be from within rather than from without. Each worker seemed to be self-motivated in his work. Paul Scudamore stresses that all employees are encouraged to think as hard as they can about their work and to pass on any great thoughts they may have. He frankly asks men and women to think and work 'beyond the call of duty' (his phrase). There seemed, however, to be no tension, no overstrain. People were apparently acting naturally, enjoying hard work and lots of it. Susie Allen was from the United States. She said that she personally enjoyed the pressure at Netherton, and that she had always enjoyed pressure. Some people at Netherton sometimes work on into the evening. They scarcely seem to have much of a lunch hour. On Friday evenings they close down religiously at 6pm and go off to drink together at a local public house. Employees were encouraged to keep away from work at week-ends. If they did not care for this kind of work and for this sort of close co-operation, new employees were assisted to leave quite quickly. Most new employees stayed.

I am trying to show how people naturally enjoy work, given decent conditions. Yet I know as well as others know, that in real life scarcely a day goes by without a person or persons being heard complaining about work. I am concerned to show that very often, in very many cases, this is a pose. A person says what others say, says what seems to be expected of him. The real and deep unhappiness of those who lack work is the best involuntary tribute to the human value of work. Let me sketch a few pictures of real persons doing real work, mostly work a good deal less interesting and less rewarding than that at Jaguar Cars and Netherton Farm. Let them be heard quietly, sometimes stutteringly, testifying to what work means to them.

Tony Hillsdon was fifty when he died in 1985. He was formerly a keen shop steward; he used to be a member of the Labour Party. When I talked to him, he had 'forsaken politics for football'. He had never been an extremist. He believed profoundly in moral values; he was not a church-goer, but believed that those values are primarily to be found in the Bible. He tried, he said, to live by them. He was a family man, working very hard in his spare time at organizing schoolboy football. He refereed at week-ends. He worked for twenty-three years at 'Cambridge Exhausts' who made (and make) radiators, exhausts and other car parts. He spent twelve years there chromium-plating. Then he had a chance to change to another shop; he learned other jobs, primarily press-operating. He said that work in a factory is very educational (in many ways). He added that you need a change from time to time. He said that 'to a large degree' he enjoyed the work, despite the fact that it was 'mundane and repetitive'. His reasons for leaving Exhausts a few years ago I shall explain in chapter 9. They were not really connected with the work itself. He became a full-time promoter for a football club. He says that 'sometimes at Exhausts we were doing twelve or thirteen hundred pieces an hour for so many hours a day'. He said that 'it could be soul-destroying if you allowed it to be'. He took care that it did not destroy his soul. He explained that if you did a certain job for three or four years you achieved a certain standard.

'It couldn't be better,' he said. 'If you're doing press-work, for example, you achieve a certain rhythm. You sail through it. You become so competent that you don't have to try. It's just second nature. You master the art, and then you need not think about it.' Then, he explained, you had time. You had time to think of other things. He said that time, of course, was fatal, unless you did things with it. 'Sometimes', he said, 'we just did crosswords'. But he added that 'every man must do something constructive'. He did a lot of thinking at his work. He said that it is important for every man to keep mentally alive. You like to feel, at the end of the day, that you have produced something. He himself had certainly kept mentally alive. He did not leave the factory because he had been mentally dying. Indeed he had for long been happy enough at 'Exhausts', because on a routine job he had had the chance to think. He had enjoyed that vastly.

I am trying to say that the legend that work on a production line is necessarily 'soul-destroying' is ill-founded. Tony's frank and honest talks with me (for he lived around the corner from me) drove my mind back to JAC Brown on *The Social Psychology of Industry* (1954). He wrote:

When a worker does a job which requires concentration and skill he may (other things being equal) perform it as a craft, and he is not bored. But what is even more important, because less obvious, is that when a worker does a job which is almost entirely automatic, boredom will not arise provided that the situation permits day-dreaming, conversation, and social distractions to take place. When a job of this type is properly arranged so that the worker realizes its significance, feels that the job is valuable, and can also engage in conversation with his or her comrades, the situation is in no respect different from that of the primitive farmer planting his crops, pulling out weeds, or the woman washing the family laundry in the river.

. . . The points we have just made are immensely important in the present context, since they show that a good deal of nonsense is spoken abut the dangers of mass-production in destroying the creative impulses of the worker.[8]

Professor Brown had experience and talked sense.

So Tony was happy enough at Exhausts (until, as we shall see, management began to change its style). 'Those outside interests', he said, 'are of paramount interest to the working man, even if it's just playing darts.' 'You have to do some forward thinking,' he said. 'You need to have something to achieve.' His soul was not killed on a job he did not have to think about. Here was an intelligent man doing a relatively dull and undemanding job. Yet he was a basically satisfied man, so long as relationships were good and his mind active. That mind at work and outside work became more and more occupied with boys' football. This may not have been ideal; it was certainly neither unworthy nor unsatisfying to him.

Matthew is a postman, young, bespectacled, with five O levels. His job is not exciting, but he quite enjoys it. He says that this is so because it gives him opportunity for thought. 'I do a lot of thinking,' he tells me. The point I am trying to underline is that an intelligent person doing a rather dull job can achieve genuine satisfaction. This is because he recognizes that the job needs to be done and also because the nature of the job often permits his mind to be occupied with thought-demanding projects. There are no doubt workers with less active minds on production lines. There are less active minds, and many of them are abundantly satisfied with dull jobs. The work of selecting for such jobs is of great importance. It is not to be left to an unimaginative supervisor. I have heard Tony Williamson, the priest-worker at British Leyland, Cowley, strongly defend work on the production line. I am still putting the case for work as a humanizing factor, as part of the fulfilment of man, even if the work happens to be dull.

We turn now to 'Derek', a younger man living with his widowed father in the Rhonnda Valley. When I saw him first, he was, at nineteen, unemployed. He hated unemployment, hated to wake up in the morning and realize that there was no work for him to go to, no reason for him to get out of bed. After leaving school, he had gone to the local College of Further Education, had taken his City and Guilds Engineering examinations. He claims to have been top student. Then he did a seven month Youth Opportunities Programme course in Telecommunications. He said that this was 'YOP at its best'. He went out daily on the job with a telephone engineer and felt that he had the job at his fingertips. To install a telephone, he said, you pick a pair of wires from the rack in the Exchange. You 'trace them out' to 'the cab', the green box on the side of the road. Then you call on the customer. Then you put a ladder on the pole to see if anything is obstructing the wire. Then you go back to the cab, install the phone in the house, run the wire to the window or door, and connect the outside wire which runs to the pole. Then you connect the wires from the Exchange to the pole and test them at the Exchange. Inside the Exchange the lines are connected by another engineer to the electronic equipment. All this was part of him, part of his mind, part of his real life, part of his mind in unemployment. This was what unemployment prevented him from doing, prevented him from being. In the meantime, by day and by night, he worked for and in the Church's 'Disco'. The Disco was for youngsters, many of them out of work. If Derek won the Pools, like my miner friends (of whom I write in various places in this book), he would still want to work, he said. He would invest the money and work on (if he could get a job). Indeed he had already, unemployed though he was, £800 in the bank, he said. He would go to Saudi Arabia if there were a job, any job, he could do there. People were inclined to smile at him. They thought he talked too much. I thought that he really wanted to work and that he really knew his telecommunications work. Now he has got the job he wanted, and he is in the Rhonnda Valley he loves. Now he is a telecommunications engineer. I would be happy to have Derek work on my telephone. He lives for a purpose, a satisfied worker. He is redeemed from the misery of unemployment.

Let me go on to write of three more ordinary persons who have found a considerable measure of satisfaction in their work. They are being, I believe, fulfilled in it. 'Mike' is a partner in a small but busy garage where repairs and servicing are carried out. The high standard of workmanship of both partners attracts customers from all over Oxford. I saw the partners out on the Ring Road on the other side of Oxford recently. They were getting a car onto the road again. They looked happy, busy being themselves, hard-working satisfied men. They are greatly liked and respected. 'Mike' is a married man with four children. When he has time at week-ends he enjoys decorating his home. One must understand (and he says it) that he would not enjoy that decoration half as much if he were unemployed and had all the time in the world in which to do it. It would not be for him 'a real job'. Anyone can decorate a house, he (quite mistakenly) thinks. 'A real job' for him is that of a garage mechanic. That establishes his identity; day by day, hour by hour, he works on; he is fulfilled. He knows what he is, is what he does. Many housewives (not all) would like 'a real job', out of the home. It need not necessarily be paid; it could be voluntary. Some women feel that somehow they are not fulfilling themselves unless they work, part-time at least, outside their own homes. That is for real. That is how some people are. 'Mike' is a perfectionist. He gets satisfaction out of work well done. He hates careless work. He was once a supervisor at British Leyland, Cowley, but he did not care for not being allowed personally to work on the vehicles. Sometimes, he says that work was held up because there was no one around to make a decision (for example, on a night shift). Sometimes parts were needed, and no one seemed to be able to obtain them. Frustrated workers, he says, begin to lose interest. He does not care to be at work and not working. When a customer wants to talk, 'Mike' may well listen but go on working. There are relationships at that garage, relationships among those who work and with those whom they serve. I was proud to be asked to do a little job for Mike's partner. When Mike was at Cowley, he was proud of helping to launch a fine new 'Princess' model. He believes strongly that people ought to be, and can be motivated at work. He does not believe that money is the chief motivator. I have heard my Durham miner friends say the same thing when they are talking quietly among themselves. We shall hear them speak a little later in this book. They like to talk about their work. The unemployed person tends to keep to himself. He has nothing much to talk about; only sometimes something to be violent about.

Young 'Richard', formerly the apprentice at the garage, worked with the partners. He is twenty-three now and has left. He is a good and keen mechanic, enjoys novel and challenging work, is bored by the servicing of cars (but does the job well). He did his initial training under a first-rate mechanic. Unfortunately, this mechanic was not always around, had other irons in the fire. Young Richard did not appreciate that. He did not like being left on his own, because he was keen to learn. At seventeen, he wanted someone to learn from more than he wanted responsibility. Anyhow, he was not being paid properly, and he knew it. He went on working but with bad grace. He knew that he was not being justly treated. When he came to the partners' garage, he learned a great deal. 'It's been pretty good ever since,' he said. 'On the whole I enjoy it,' he added. He knew the partners worked hard; he knew they did jobs conscientiously. He said that the partners would 'bend over backwards to help anyone'. He recalled that other (and bigger) garage he used to work at. He says that 'they covered up there', turned out bad work looking good. He did not care for that. In fact, he would have nothing to do with it. He says that they got rid of a man who did jobs properly. He says that they patched jobs up, did not really want to know their customers' problems. He must have been an awkward apprentice to have around. He was not satisfied. Eventually they got rid of him. He was too conscientious a worker, too honest a person. At work at the partners' he was fulfilled. I would tremble for what would happen if he were unemployed. He is working (hard) in Israel now. Hard work suits him.

'Alan' is a chiropodist. He did various other jobs before he learned this one. He works fast. He knows he is needed, and he likes to be needed. He believes that rioting and vandalism take place, because young people sometimes feel they are not needed. People, he says, need to be 'stretched' at their work. The unemployed, he thinks, gain some joy in the midst of their misery, in long protest marches. They are glad, he thinks, to have tired feet from honest marching if they cannot have them from honest work. He believes that hard work is part of the quality of life. He says that if circumstances compelled him to give up his present job, he would try to learn another one quickly. I think I understand what he means about the unemployed. They must have something to do. They cannot march all the time.

'Nicky' is forty, but looks much younger. He works for a firm of architectural model-makers. He likes work. If he had to change his job he would 'probably get to like another job'. He is a committed Christian, but he says that his work is nothing to do with his Christianity. That is a common enough view. He says that work means 'belonging'. He says that he likes to see people pleased with his work, and when they are pleased he works harder. That is how he is, he says. With a job, he has an identity, is a person. Without one, he would have little identity. He would be nobody. That is his opinion.

What is left of this chapter is concerned with youngsters in the Rhonnda Valley (where 'Derek' came from). 'Carl' is twenty-one. He has finished his four-year apprenticeship. He has a disturbed background, although there is loving security for him now. However, he remains erratic, unpredictable. He is not pleased with himself. He says ruefully, 'I like work, but not too much of it.' He says, 'I don't like long hours, with overtime'. Perhaps this is natural enough, anyhow for Carl. Yet he went on 'I wouldn't like to have time on my hands. I think most people have got it in them to work. It's part of them'. He gives a good part of his spare time to helping with the famous Disco. He says that he does not think that he would bother with this if he were out of work. He means that he would lose heart without work. He would feel that he had not only nothing to do but nothing to give. His job was the making of him (when I last saw him).

Lastly, let us look at Rhonnda Enterprises at Porth in mid-Glamorgan. It was founded to provide work and basic training in skills for young unemployed persons who had had six months or more of unemployment It pre-dates the current Youth Training Scheme, and was funded by the Manpower Services Commission with aid from the EEC European Social Fund. When I visited it, it was well staffed, with keen, competent, devoted management and supervisors. It aimed to equip and assist youngsters towards permanent employment. They might have as long as two years of training there. Simon had only been working there for three days when I saw him. He was learning electronics. He had the first tool he had ever made in his hand, when he came to talk to me. His eyes shone; he had great hopes and plans for the future; he was proud to be associated with an enterprise which was doing 'real' work and producing and selling goods which were really needed. His family was shortly to go on holiday; he had decided that he preferred to stay at work. 'John' was older and would shortly finish his one year's training. He 'would go anywhere,' he said.

24

He wanted to keep his mind occupied. 'I don't want to become lazy,' he said quietly to me. I heard afterwards that he was not a steady worker. He was talking perhaps more of the lad he would like to be than of the lad he really was. Somewhere, somehow, perhaps something had gone wrong in his development. I felt, however, as I saw boy after boy, that John was the exception to the rule. Here, on the whole, were the seeming failures, the potentially long-term unemployed, acquiring skills under the best possible auspices, finding themselves, in process of fulfilment. But the Valley was full of those who were finding nothing, just passing the time. Only hope kept them smiling.

NOTES

1 *Job Satisfaction*, 1982, p.23.
2 Wildwood House, 1975, p. xii (first published 1972).
3 Pelican, 1968, p. 273.
4 *Op.Cit.* pp. 4-5.
5 T. Nichols and H. Beynon, Routledge and Kegan Paul, 1977.
6 *Workers, (op. cit.)*, p. xii.
7 ibid, p. 12.
8 Penguin, 1980, p. 207 (first published 1954).

3

Protestant Work Ethic

In my continuing implied attack upon the tolerance of mass unemployment in our midst, I am concerned to promote the conception of work, of purposeful activity of social significance, as a fulfilling, a humanizing factor. Because of this, I am accused of believing in what is commonly known as the Protestant (or Calvinist) Work Ethic. In fact, I do not hold this at all. I shall try to show that I dissociate myself from it. I am, of course, obliged to admit that the Work Ethic itself lives on (despite my lack of support for it). From the pulpit of St Lawrence Jewry church on 5 May 1981, no less a person than the Prime Minister of the United Kingdom of Great Britain and Northern Ireland herself declared that it was in a Christian home that she had learned that creating wealth is a Christian obligation. She seemed to the *Guardian* reporter, Dennis Barker, to be saying that work was 'not only a necessity, but a duty and a virtue'.[1] I shall attempt in this chapter to distinguish what John Calvin said from what is commonly held to be the Protestant Work Ethic. I believe indeed that work is important to man, is fulfilling to him, actually plays a part (as we shall see in chapter 5) in his salvation. However, I am writing of the work itself, and by no means of any reward which that may bring to the worker (other than his self-fulfilment). The fulfilling, saving work which he does may well leave him a poor and (from a worldly point of view) unrewarded man. It will, however, help to leave him a satisfied person. This is something quite different from the Protestant Work Ethic.

Eric Fromm, the German-American psycho-analyst and sociologist, writes with anger of 'Puritan ethics, with the emphasis on work . . . as evidence of goodness'. He claims that 'man has accepted the contents of the Calvinistic doctrine while rejecting its religious formulation'. He says that 'for the last few centuries Western man has been obsessed by the idea of work, by the need for constant activity'. He claims that modern society teaches that man's aim in life must be 'fulfilment of his duty to work', that all human energy must be 'canalized' into work. All this, he says, is 'the meaning of work as it developed in the centuries following the Reformation, especially under the influence of Calvinism'.[2]

There are indeed grounds for accusing post-Reformation society of over-valuing work. As this book develops, I hope to show that it is quite wrong to promote or tolerate work which is too hard or which goes on too long, work which is exhausting. One reads today with astonishment the panegyric concerning the early twentieth century English working man written by C. F. G. Masterman, a young Liberal Member of Parliament, later to become a Cabinet Minister. Masterman rented a tenement flat in Albany Buildings in Camberwell, in South London. He was a Guardian of the Poor and a worker for the Children's Holiday Fund. Living amongst factory and laundry workers, he was respected by all classes and was regarded as an acute and penetrating observer. His *Condition of England*[3] went into six editions within two years. Although he knew the unsatisfactory conditions under which many people lived and worked, he was able to write that 'in such surroundings and despite such drawbacks, there labours a hardy race of men, whose efforts in skill, perseverance, and indefatigable industry, have earned them supremacy in the markets of the world'. He referred with admiration to 'the invincible patience of the English workman', who 'will endure almost anything – . . . in silence . . . until it becomes unendurable'.[4] His version of the Protestant Work Ethic is an echo of that of Thomas Carlyle in the previous century:

> All work, even cotton-spinning, is noble; work is alone noble; be that here said and asserted once more. Show me a people energetically busy; heaving, struggling, all shoulders at the wheel; their heart pulsing, every muscle swelling, with man's energy and will; . . . I show you a people of whom great good is already predictable; to whom all manner of good is yet certain, if their energy endure.[5]

While again dissociating myself from this sort of apology for what was sometimes no less than sweated labour, let us look into the religious foundations of such thinking. Arthur Exell, author of *The Politics of the Production Line*,[6] worked at Oxford Radiators between 1929 and 1975 and suffered persecution there because of his political views. He is a thoroughly honest man. He describes himself as having worked hard, long and cheerfully all his time there. He tells me that he worked this way because this was his duty to God, as he had learned it amongst his Welsh Baptist family where his father was a lay preacher in the Rhonnda Valley. He is a Communist now, but in no way denies or regrets his Christian upbringing. That upbringing amidst the Welsh Baptists included the inculcation of the Protestant Work Ethic.

This Work Ethic, as we have seen, is sometimes called 'the Calvinist Work Ethic'. Let us consider briefly how justifiable this title is. Max Weber, in his famous *Protestant Work Ethic and The Spirit of Capitalism*, declared that the 'works of Calvin' provide, amongst other phenomena, the starting point for 'the relationship between the old Protestant work ethic and the spirit of capitalism'.[7] Yet in fact Calvin warned his hearers and readers against the dangers of riches, exhorting them to place neither their hearts nor their trust in them and to esteem 'the simple blessing of God more than the whole world'. He added that they were to take any gain which should come to them 'as from the hand of God'. Despite this, there is little in his *Institution* which resembles the later form of the Protestant Work Ethic. He writes magisterially, with biblical knowledge and insight, with great wisdom. He tells us that 'we are the stewards of everything God has conferred on us by which we are able to help our neighbour and are required to render account of our stewardship'.[8] Our efforts are to be directed towards God. He tells us that those who do not so direct them 'may possibly toil and labour a great deal, but they are really only wandering about in endless circuits, without making any progress'. He writes that all that we receive from God must be employed in his service. To be an authentic man, fulfilled and in full possession of his humanity, according to Calvin, 'the human being must work in the faith and obedience due to God'.[9] Work, he tells us, is one element in human vocation. 'It is necessary then that each human being accomplish the work God gives him, that he encourages himself towards it and satisfies himself in it'.[10] He asks that 'we demonstrate by our lives that we have not in vain been designed by God'. He writes quite splendidly that 'to act is to range oneself in everything alongside the action of God'.[11] He says reasonably enough, 'Of course the fields are to be tilled, we must sweat over the gathering-in of the fruits of the earth, each must undergo and endure the labour of his calling . . .'.[12]

He wrote wisely that we should 'exercise such care (in work) as is a mean between a soft nonchalance and the torment of excessive zeal, by means of which the unbelievers kill themselves'.[13] Of course, he condemned idleness. So did the Catholic Church condemn the capital sin of sloth. Calvin wrote, sensibly enough, that 'God gives each person some charge and exercise so that he shall not lie idly'.[14]

Let us consider seriously, as we must, not what the great Calvin taught, but what lesser theologians (and others) wrote during the course of the development of that Protestant Work Ethic which sometimes bears his name. A. Biéler is emphatic that Weber and others have confused the message of John Calvin 'with that of religious movements of Calvinist origin but already deformed and secularized'. 'One has not the right', he says, 'to assimilate the Calvinism of Calvin with later Puritanism.'[15] John Bunyan (1628-1688) wrote during the 1660s *The Heavenly Footman* (or *A Description of the Man that gets to Heaven*). It included an 'Epistle to all the Slothful and Careless People'. It is a tract against sloth. He writes:

> He that is slothful is loth to set about the Work he should follow. He doth his Work by the Halves. Would you be willing to be damned for Slothfulness? . . . God will not be slothful or negligent to damn you.
>
> First, I beseech you in the Name of our Lord Jesus Christ, that none of you do run so lazily in the Way of Heaven as to hinder either yourselves or others. . . . You see here, that he that will go to Heaven must run for it: Yea, . . . continually, to strip off every Thing that would hinder in his Race, with the Rest.[16]

In 1684, Richard Steele wrote his *Trades-man's Calling*. He explains that man's calling, his work, is to rescue him from the sin which inevitably accompanies idleness. 'He that is fully employed, hath not that Leisure to sin that others have . . . he that is without a Calling is liable to Satan's Temptation . . . Tho you have no Outward Necessity to inforce you to take up a Calling, yet it may be necessary for you, in respect of your Soul, to prevent the Corruptions that are apt to breed there. The Standing Pool is prone to Putrefaction.'[17] Early in the next century, Isaac Watts would be writing in *Divine Songs for Children:*

> In works of labour, or of skill,
> I would be busy too;

For Satan finds some mischief still
for idle hands to do.

One cannot help but suspect and reject the theology and ethics of one who could also write in *Divine Songs in Easy Language for the Use of Children* (1715):

Have ye not heard what dreadful plagues
Are threatened by the Lord?
To him that breaks his father's law
Or mocks his mother's word?
The ravens shall pick out his eyes
And eagles eat the same.

In 1719, soon after (according to him) 'the great and wonderful Event of the Protestant Succession', John Sewter wrote *How to be Wise and Wealthy*. He tells us that wisdom and wealth are the two things that most men covet and which are most likely to make them happy in this world. 'The right Use of them', he assures us 'will dispose us for the Felicities of a better.'[18] Indeed the sub-title of his book is: 'Industry and Frugality, as the due and regular Exercise thereof is the necessary Means of procuring the Happiness of This Life, and preparing for that of a better'. He contrasts industry, activity, 'dispatch' in business, of the kind that creates wealth, with that 'slothful, lazy, unactive Spirit' that loves ease and has 'an Aversion to Work'.[19] He explains this as 'a mighty Propensity to Ease and Recess, . . . a Habit of Sauntering and Littleness, that the least Attendance on Business and the necessary Affairs of Life is most disagreeable and irksome'. 'This', he tells us, 'is generated and produced from a careless unconcerned Temper, that is in no wise inclined to forecast and be solicitious to prevent Evil, or to procure good Events; but so supine and thoughtless, as to Future Things, as tho' we were to be fed and provided for by Miracle, as the *Israelites* were with *Manna*.' All this, he assures us, is 'the Reverse to an *industrious* active Mind, the Consideration whereof may be of great Use to give us a more perfect Idea of the Excellency of this inestimable Virtue of Industry'.[20] He goes on to reassure us that those who care for small concerns 'upon Earth' 'shall receive their Reward in the other at the Hands of their bountiful Lord and Master'.[21] So, in winning the world the Christian also wins the salvation of his

31

soul. 'Plunged in the cleansing waters of later Puritanism, the qualities which less enlightened ages had denounced as social vices emerged as economic virtues,' writes R. H. Tawney. He added that 'they emerged as moral virtues as well'.[22]

This 'blessed' capacity to make money, these moral virtues result (according to the Ethic) in that wealth for individual and for nation which is the sign of God's approval. William Wood, writing *A Survey of Trade* in 1718,[23] declares: 'The Almighty has so established the Necessities of Mankind . . . that there is scarce any Man, not disabled by Nature or Accident, but may by Industry and Pains, earn more than would supply his Necessities.' One thinks of the struggles of many in the Third World, of hard work often done by weak bodies (as I have seen it being done in Bangladesh, for example). One feels ashamed of such statements being made in the name of 'the Almighty'. We read William Cobbett who writes that 'abundant living . . . is . . . the surest basis of national greatness and security'.[24] We recoil surely from a theory that implies that in poor African and South American communities there is no basis for 'greatness and security'. We recoil even from the statement of the good John Wesley to the effect that religion must lead to industry and frugality and these in turn to riches.[25] The Protestant Work Ethic has come to be associated not only with hard work but also with money-making.

In my distaste for the Protestant Work Ethic in its developed forms, I am not alone. *Industrial and Commercial Training* is a respected journal, and those who write in it write seriously. In its September 1981 number, a writer declared:

> One of the mainsprings of society's attitude to work, wealth and reward is the Protestant work ethic. . . . Calvin's followers gradually came to regard growing trade, as well as the wealth it produced, as an indication of God's favour. It led man to see wealth as a blessing from God, and the unequal distribution of material goods as a matter of divine providence.[26]

This kind of thing is what the Protestant Work Ethic has come to mean in many people's minds.

The Work Ethic needs in fact to be disowned by Christians if they are to help to promote the attack upon unemployment which is needed. Work is necessary for human beings not to win the favour and the rewards of God, but to enable man to fulfil himself through purposeful activity of social significance. The Protestant Work Ethic, as it is generally understood, misleads concerning work. 'The Church', says a writer in *The Observer* of 31st May 1981, 'has used the work ethic for hundreds of years now to keep the working masses in their place.' She adds that the church has become an 'instrument of a society geared to the profit motive', and declares that the Protestant Work Ethic has to be 'changed from within'. The Bishop of Hereford in his April 1981 *Diocesan Magazine* assumed the Protestant Work Ethic to mean that a person works out his salvation by the sweat of his brow. This is a parody of what John Calvin taught. I am entirely opposed to any doctrine that seems to sanction any kind of over-work, any work that exhausts. At a time when the work available is limited and the number of unemployed workers large, let work be done conscientiously but in moderation. In chapter 10 I shall indeed make some suggestions for the sharing of work. I denounce a work ethic which seems to suggest that work necessarily sanctifies and that it gains heavenly reward. I am horrified when none other than ex-President Richard Nixon declares that 'the work ethic holds that labour is good in itself, that a man becomes a better person by the act of working'. Yet I shall try to show in chapter 5 that, although hard work does not by itself save man, work is an element in that process which culminates in that human fulfilment which we call salvation. I am completely in accord with any doctrine that teaches that man's vocation is to change the environment, to be actively creative. In this society of ours in which mass unemployment is one of its most prominent and utterly lamentable features, it is vital that the limited opportunities for creatively changing the environment be shared out amongst all capable of working.

NOTES

1 *The Guardian,* 6 March 1981, p. 1.
2 *Man for Himself,* Routledge and Kegan Paul, 1975, pp. 81, 134-5, 108, 19, 148, 194 (1st published in UK, 1949).
3 Methuen, 1960 edition, ed. J. T. Boulton (1st published 1909).
4 ibid., p. 16.
5 *Chartism Past and Present,* Chapman and Hall, p. 221.
6 History Workshop Journal Pamphlet, 1981.
7 *The Protestant Ethic and the Spirit of Capitalism,* George Unwin, 1965, p. 75 (1st published 1904-5).
8 *Institutes of the Christian Religion* III, 7, 5 (originally published 1559).
9 *Calvin's Commentaries,* ed. D. W. and T. F. Torrance, St Andrew Press, 1972, *St Matthew* 6, 25.
10 A. Biéler: *La Pensée Economique de Calvin,* Lib. de l'Université George et Cie., Geneva, 1959, p. 403.
11 *Commentaries (op. cit.), Colossians* I, 10.
12 ibid., *St Matthew* 6, II.
13 ibid., *St Matthew* 6, 25.
14 ibid., *St Matthew* 20, I.
15 *La Pensée Economique (op. cit.),* pp. 494-5.
16 E. Johnston, Ludgate Street, 1774, pp. VII and X.
17 Samual Sprint, 1684, p. 19.
18 Philip Bishop, Exeter, 1716, p. 20.
19 ibid., p. 23.
20 ibid., p. 24.
21 ibid., p. 94.
22 *Religion and the Rise of Capitalism,* John Murray, 1926, p. 249.
23 W. Wilkins at Dryden's Head under the Royal Exchange, p. I.
24 *Cottage Economy,* C. Clement, Fleet Street, 1822, p. 4.
25 M. Weber: *The Protestant Ethic (op. cit.),* p. 157.
26 p. 302.

4

Work in Ancient Greece (and Elsewhere)

I am engaged in attacking as strongly as I can the continuing toleration of mass unemployment in Britain (and elsewhere). However, I am also saying that the chief reason why unemployment is so degrading is that an unemployed person is normally deprived by worklessness of that work which is natural and fulfilling to him. When I say this, I am sometimes accused of propagating the Protestant Work Ethic. I have replied to this. However, I am also accused of ignoring both the happiness (and fulfilment) of the ancient Greeks, who are supposed to have left all manual labour to the slaves, and the alleged contentment of others whose needs appear to be satisfied without their having to work. I am thinking of gypsies and of 'happy savages' and of the retired.

Let me now direct attention to the ancient Greece of the 5-4 centuries BC. Here it is commonly believed that there was a state of dignified and cultured non-working life for the free. Free men did not work; in fact they despised honest work and left it to the slaves. Distinguished men have accepted this misreading of ancient history, and distinguished men continue to propagate it. If it were true, it would be evidence for the theory that man does not need to work, that he can find fulfilment in leisure pursuits (including politics). There would be a measure of truth in such a theory if to be a worker meant merely to do physical work or to be in paid employment. I have tried to make it plain that to work is not necessarily to have a paid job. Rather it is to change by some means the environment, to pursue an activity towards a social end. A person can work with his head, can work hard without exerting his hands or feet. The teacher works hard with mind and lips, the writer with pen and type-writer. Both grow (as we say) 'desperately' tired, as the work goes on. The politician may be a very hard worker as he stumps about the country using his voice (and dictating his letters and making his pastoral calls). The professional tennis player or footballer can work hard at his game. Even the aristocratic landowner can work diligently at the supervision of work on his estate.

35

Let us look hard at the allegation that the ancient Greeks did not work. In 1937, in *The Divine Imperative*, the distinguished theologian Emil Brunner wrote: 'The Athenian citizen, especially if he was a philosopher, did not work; that was the business of slaves and manual workers. Work . . . is a degrading affair, which should be avoided as far as possible.'[1] He is saying what has been said before (and since). What he is saying has been authoritatively contradicted by various authorities. Despite these authorities, as late as 1977, Professor Anthony Dyson can write of 'the Greek lack of esteem for work', of work as justified only 'as a means of buying the opportunity for contemplation'.[2] The seriousness for my thesis of this alleged Greek contempt for work is considerable. If men so wise as the great Greek philosophers of the 5-4 centuries BC considered that work was degrading, this is surely a blow for my claim that work is humanly fulfilling and necessary.

It is interesting that in fact the ancient Greeks really had no theory of work, no strong views whatsoever about it. There is nowhere in Greek literature any trace of an ideology of work. The Greeks had no concept of work as an important human function. For the Greeks there were different occupations, jobs to be done. 'Work never acquired for the Greeks positive intrinsic value'.[3] What mattered for the Greeks were the conditions under which the jobs were done. It is true that, with Aristotle and later philosophers, an element of intellectual snobbery does begin to appear. Aristotle writes: 'It is noble not to practise any sordid craft, since it is the mark of a free man not to live at another's beck and call.'[4] However, it is not work but subservience which he is derogating. I must add that he says more (and worse). He writes of slaves as 'slaves by nature', as 'belonging to others by nature'.[5] I regret the remark. However, Messrs Austin and Vidal-Maquet tell us that we must see in these ideas only the reflection of aristocratic prejudices and the dreams of reactionary philosophers.[6] Professor Kitto puts the record straight, makes it clear that such remarks are not truly representative of the mind of the philosophers, the thinking of the Greeks. He tells us that in the later Greek world there were indeed philosophers and writers who wrote with scorn about work. But theirs, he explains, was 'a split world'.[7] They were not typical of Greek philosophy.

It certainly remains untrue to say of the Athenian citizen that he did not work and that he regarded work as degrading. Solon in his *Laws* (of the early 8th century BC) had written that every father must teach his son a trade.[8] According to Xenophon, the great Socrates, a stone-cutter by profession, would drift into work-shops and studios to talk to the workers about their trade.[9] Greek citizens, owners of small farms, would work happily in their fields, so long as they could go off to perform their duties in the Assembly when required.[10] Where there was democracy in Greece, there was hard work in politics. The citizen worked with his body in the fields and went on to the Assembly to work with his mind. Citizens were taught by the philosophers to keep themselves fit for the things of the mind. Man, as Aristotle told us, is a political animal,[11] a person associated with a state. Man must be a thoughtful citizen. The Greeks esteemed greatly 'the high-minded man', 'the man of great soul'. Of course, the 'political animal' must not wear himself out, 'make himself inferior'[12] by his work. He must not exhaust his body and thereby incapacitate his mind. However, Professor Finley declares that 'the majority of the free men, even of the free citizens, worked for their livelihood'.[13] They got on with their jobs.

Behind the assumption concerning alleged Greek contempt for work lies the common belief that ancient Greece had a basically slave economy. Professor Finley tells us that we cannot be at all sure concerning the number of slaves at any one time in Greece.[14] However, there is an abundance of evidence to the effect that free men and slaves worked alongside one another in the fields. Xenophon, in his mid-fourth century *Memorabilia*, wrote that those who can buy slaves do so in order to have companions at work.[15] We know that both slaves and free men worked on the building of the Acropolis above Athens. Simias, a mason, worked with five slaves on the Erechtheum, the temple on the Acropolis; all were apparently paid at the same rate. It was a drachma a day. There were altogether eighty-six workmen, of whom twenty were slaves.[16] Thomas Wiedemann, of the Department of Classics and Archaeology at Bristol, writes to me that 'it is a nineteenth century idea that in the ancient world the slaves constituted a sort of working class'. He adds: 'It was not the case, either in Greece or Rome, that certain kinds of work were reserved to slaves because they were risky, dirty or dangerous. . . In fact, we find free workers prepared to do any work . . . so the simple distinction made by Marxists and many Liberals between slaves who did the work, and free men who practised a life of leisure, won't do.'

It was Juvenal at the beginning of the second century AD who wrote of 'mens sana in corpore sano', of a healthy mind in a healthy body. We probably know more than Aristotle of the right care of the body in order to care rightly for the mind. I myself was taught at the Department of Education in Oxford that a physical skill was often a help to the skill of the mind. I shall be saying in the last chapter that eight hours of physical work in a factory is too hard, too tiring for the good working of the mind. The tired worker shrugs off politics in a way that an Athenian citizen working on his farm would have been ashamed to do. I have tried to show here that the Greeks, who tended to reject for their citizens and free men over-work and degrading work, did not otherwise think about work at all; certainly they did not despise it. 'The peasant small holder who works his own land is a symbol of freedom for both Greeks and Romans', Thomas Wiedemann writes to me. Professor Kitto assures us that slaves were 'certainly not the basis of the economic life of Attica', that some Greek citizens' homes had no slaves at all. Indeed, he says, the simplicity of Greek living did not call for them.[17]

We conclude with the testimony of two scholars. Professor Sir Alfred Zimmern dismisses as 'a false idea' the common assumption that the Greeks regarded manual work as degrading.[18] The Greeks, he said, never recognized any distinction between a craft or 'trade' and a 'profession'.[19] He claimed that in ancient Greece art, literature, philosophy and all other great products of the nation's genius were 'sturdily rooted, and find continued nourishment, in the broad common soil of national life'.[20] G. Glotz tells us that (among free Greeks) there were no rigid divisions. The classes, he says, mixed together in national life. He refers to the obligation of work as 'that law of Zeus that Hesiod used to preach to the peasants, saying that Socrates contrasted this favourably with the inactivity of those who dream'. He quotes from 'the new comedy', that 'interpreter of popular sentiment': 'It does not matter how you earn your living, so long as you commit no shabby action.'[21] Livings had to be earned, and work physical or mental was part of the life of the ancient Greek. The importance of work for a person's full development may not have been realized; but work was certainly not despised.

It has also been suggested (in opposition to my thesis) that on tropical islands and elsewhere simple people have lived happily without working for their living. Coconuts and mangoes have dropped, as it were, into their mouths. The poet Dryden wrote in the 17th century:

Ere the base laws of servitude began,
When wild in woods the noble savage ran

The noble savage in fact ran because he was busy hunting. Red Indian tribes vary immensely in their customs and habits. Canals had been built by them in the arid west of America as early as 1000 AD. Along the Rio Grande in New Mexico lived the Pueblos who built fortified cities, including buildings four storeys high. Here men laboured in the fields with their digging sticks and hoes, while the women made handsomely painted pottery in many colours. The men hunted rabbits, throwing clubs at them to kill them. They wove in winter, making cotton clothing with varied patterns, white kilts with black and red borders. They did basket work, making trays and dishes and even cradles. There were times for planting, for harvesting, for 'teaching the boys the system of things'.[22] Amongst some tribes, women worked in the fields while men hunted. The women raised maize, beans, squash, pumpkins. For the men, the early spears came to be supplemented by bows and arrows. Men made pottery for cooking, jars and bowls for the storage of grain. Some of their clay pottery was burnished with stone to assume a brightly polished effect.

The Anthropological Museum at the University of British Columbia at Vancouver provides not only a magnificent display of Indian crafts, but a challenge to modern Indians to resume their craft work. Indeed some of them are doing exactly that today in the Museum. One sees examples of modern Indian crafts, as well as of Indian work of earlier times. There are enormous and elaborately carved and painted totems, sometimes incorporated in wooden dwelling huts. There are exquisite carved figures of birds, beasts, whales. There are gorgeous head-dresses of wood and shell, masks for wearing at festival dancing, blankets, shawls, kilts, mantas, sashes, moccasins, decorated cotton skirts, the work of Indians of yesterday and today.

The Indian at work in his own way, in his own time, is a

fulfilled person, with self-respect, identity, purposeful activity. It is tragic that many Indians have had to face not only challenge to their traditional ways of life, but to employment itself in modern western-type Canadian society. The Minister for Human Resources of the Province of British Columbia writes to me that no precise figures of Indian unemployment are available, because distinctions based upon ethnic origin are not made. However, she adds that 'it can be anticipated that they experience high levels of unemployment'. The Canadian Government Minister of Indian Affairs writes that 'use of social assistance among Indians has increased from about one third of the population to slightly more than one half in the last 10-15 years'. This, he admits, is due in part to 'high unemployment among Indians'. In *Indian Conditions: A Survey* (of 1980), the same Federal Ministry stated that 'in the absence of successful job creation, social support for increasing numbers of unemployed Indians may double over the next 10 to 15 years'. The Government is rightly disturbed.

These are depressing figures. Those who deal with Indians know that unemployment is one of the factors contributing to the unhappiness of Indian peoples whose whole way of life has been disturbed. Many of them have lost their right to work in their own way, some of them their right to work at all. No benefits offered to them make up for this. A house provided by government is no compensation for what you could have built for yourself. I know that in the north of the provinces of Alberta, Saskatchewan and Manitoba, the suicide rate amongst young Indians is pathetically high. Take his traditional working way of life away from 'the noble savage', and for him his life may not seem worth living.

The Australian Aborigine has had his traditional way of life yet more cruelly disturbed. He wants to get back to his traditional land of which he is part and with which he and his ancestors are (to him) inextricably connected. However, I have seen the Aborigine at work on cattle properties, riding as a stockman, mustering, 'brewing up', a happy man, fulfilled. His work has changed, but he has found the new work satisfying. Yet the rhythm, the work pattern of the new life, is different from that of the old. He has often not stuck at it. I have seen the same man having left his job, lost his hope and found in liquor his only consolation. The Aborigine population of Australia has until recently steadily decreased. Despite Commonwealth and State assistance in provision of land and housing and education, as well as assistance to him in unemployment, the will to live has diminished. Only 180,000 full blood Aborigines remain. The 'savage' may indeed be noble, but he tends to be unhappy. My old 'flying priest' friend, for many years in charge of a far N. Queensland mission, writes of the Aborigine in his natural condition as 'having to work hard to live'. This, of course, was true. He says that 'now that government-conferred security has come to them, the people here are content to sit and wait for the Government cheque to arrive'. He says that they are content but not happy; whereas he himself is 'terribly discontented but very happy'. He goes on to say that 'in an environment where people have nothing to do, one will inevitably find discord and a shortage of harmony, and lots of trouble-makers and so on'. He refers to any idea that the Aborigine may be happy in his state-supported condition of doing nothing as (in his vivid Australian terminology) 'bull'. An Australian National University study recently found that in New South Wales only ten per cent of the Aborigines live beyond the age of forty-nine, twenty years short of the average life expectancy of white Australians. Fifty-three per cent are unemployed.[23] Whatever other factors are at work, unemployment is certainly one of the elements contributing to the relatively short and unhappy lives of many Aborigines. The Queensland documentary film *The World about Us – Sacred Rights* was a revelation in 1985 to thousands of British television viewers. It showed land-starved people, with nothing to do, with young men dying of inanition at thirty-eight. In the New South Wales town where I worked in 1984 the Aborigines and part-Aborigines hung about all day along the main street and shopping centre. They were not conspicuous, and no one ever mentioned them. They were like ghosts, faint reminders of what they once were and of what they might have been.

Those who feel that lack of personal overseas experience renders them incapable of estimating justly the importance of work (and lack of work) in the life of Indian and Aborigine will have at least a limited experience of a 'foreign' people within Great Britain, the gypsies. The 'Romany' people originated in the Indian subcontinent, and have been in Britain for 400 years. They are sometimes known as 'the Travellers', although this title is used especially for those of Irish origin who have come to this country and who follow the gypsy way of life. Dr Thomas Acton describes the word 'traveller' as 'the most widely used and inclusive word of self- and-group-identification among gypsies in England and Wales'. He also tells us that, far from being a homogeneous group, the gypsies are a most disunited and ill-defined people, possessing a continuity, rather than a community, of culture'.[24] At any rate, the title 'traveller' stands for the strong feeling among gypsies (and others) that 'travelling' is of the essence of the gypsy life. Although some gypsies have in fact ceased to travel and have become house-dwellers, those whom I am attempting to describe and to explain are those who are nomadic, who do not settle. It is interesting anyhow that those who do take houses frequently revert to the nomadic life, so strong is the habit and the tradition of 'travelling'. Indeed, the children of gypsies born in houses often become 'travellers', as they grow up. They are, it is said, 'marked for life' by their gypsy origin. The gypsy habits and traditions seem to be easily acquired and to have a strong hold over all associated with them. Some habits seem repulsive to those who do not share them, and ordinary British citizens are inclined to judge the gypsies adversely and severely. Amongst many letters written to the Oxfordshire County Council there are references to 'the squalor they have created', their 'deplorable hygiene', their 'abuse' and their 'thieving'.[25] Those few who have taken the trouble to study the gypsies agree that this kind of comment does not give a just picture of the gypsy. Dr Acton quotes other authorities on gypsy life to assert that 'theirs is a life of their own that becomes meaningful, reasonable and normal, once you get close to it'.[26]

There is very little begging amongst gypsies these days. The impression, however, remains with the general public that they are a lazy people. This simply is not true, unless to be lazy means to have an entirely different pattern of work and relaxation from that of the hourly paid worker. Those who do not know the gypsies would be amazed to learn how hard (and fast) many of them do work. On farms, gypsies sometimes work in the fields for farmers. For the farmer (and others) they often lay tarmac. They make their contracts, sometimes undercutting the commercial contractor. They meet early in the morning at the tarmac yard to pick up their load. Often the boys of the family (who sit lightly to school) work with their fathers. They may begin work at an exceptionally early hour, and sometimes work with almost demonic speed, determined to finish as soon as possible. This is all quite different from the British way of working; it may well be no less authentic. It is easier for an Australian bushman to appreciate the gypsy, because he himself tends to work irregular hours, owing to the needs of the livestock and the circumstances of the season (including the incidence of drought). The gypsy will mend roofs for farmers (and others) and work on scrap. His wife will volunteer to tell fortunes. There is among the gypsies still some of the traditional hawking of charms and flowers, as well as of old gold and silver, of woollens and mixed rags and of 'antique furniture' as well. There are craftsmen and pedlars, agricultural workers and horsedealers amongst them. A Scottish gypsy on the radio declared of a fellow-gypsy: 'He knows no bosses, no gaffers. He could make a living out of the dirt of a man's foot. He could make money out of old rope'.

Above all, let it be clear that the gypsy chooses to be basically self-employed so that he can work in his own time and in his own way. In that way, and not in laziness, he will be happy and fulfilled. Indeed, he may have something to teach us; for we may have to adapt our traditional work patterns, in order that the unemployed shall have some work. I want also to emphasize that the gypsy's travelling (for which, of course, he is not paid) is part of his 'work'. To travel, to pack up and move, is not paid employment, but it is hard work. See the gypsy on the move. The whole family comes to life. Each member has his allotted job. The dogs bark, the horses (if there are any) neigh. The dogs in fact spring onto the vehicles at an early stage of the move, lest they be left behind. Sometimes, regrettably, they are left behind. There is much talk, but also much quick hard work. The cut glass, the Crown Derby, all has to be carefully wrapped for the journey.

The gypsy loves to drive. 'It is natural for us to move,' he explains smilingly. It is part of his purposeful activity, and it undoubtedly has social significance. I believe the pressures on the gypsy are from within, as well as the economic ones from without. That is true of all of us; we all have our pressures from within. None of us is complete economic man. In all his intermittent but purposeful activity the gypsy finds joy; in activity he is humanized. He gains satisfaction, achieves self-respect (if not the respect of the community). Travelling, working, not working:

this is his life. If he were a non-worker, as the ignorant imagine, he would not be the happy person he is. Not for him the five-day week, the eight-hour day. Perhaps some of us would be much happier (and better) in our work, if we were permitted to follow (like him) our 'natural' rhythm a little more. Some British firms are indeed experimenting where possible with allowing employees to begin at a late or an early hour so long as they work a full day. We shall consider in the last chapter, amongst other suggestions for ridding ourselves of unemployment, the possibility of more part-time work, of job-sharing, and also of work-sharing. People for whom a four-hour day brings in sufficient income may be more fulfilled than is the (sometimes) tired worker after the eight hour day. It is conceivable that a society recognizing the need of work for all may discover new and more elastic patterns of work for some. We might even learn to respect something of the gypsy mode of life (and work).

All sorts of people seem to others at one time or another to be doing no work. Very often it is only that they are doing work in a different way, according to a different rhythm. One must be careful about one's judgements. If one looks really hard at the ancient Greek, or at 'the noble savage', or at the modern gypsy, one discovers that in each case work does in fact form a considerable part of life. Work that satisfies fulfils, tends to be demanding but need not necessarily be tiring. If it is to be really satisfying, fulfilling, it is likely to be in some measure creative, of some social value, 'altering the environment'. The gypsy has a working life and is a happy person. The unemployed British, the Red Indian, the Aborigine, are unhappy beings, in so far as they lack work.

The Red Indians, the Australian Aborigines, the gypsies of Great Britain are all different peoples living in conditions different from those of their origin. They mostly suffer in different ways and degrees from up-rooting, from inevitable challenges to their traditions, from unwillingness and indeed incapacity to be assimilated to the other peoples in the midst of whom they live. I do not want to minimize the peculiar problems of such peoples. I must, however, stress that in addition to all these problems, there is amongst the Indians and the Aborigines the extra and serious problem of lack of work. I have seen Indians in jobs in eastern Canada and I have seen Indians at work on traditional crafts in British Columbia who seemed to be happy and fulfilled persons. I have come to a study of gypsies which has taught me that they maintain, on the whole, a satisfying and fulfilling life, because in their own way they keep up that purposeful activity which is the basis of what I mean by work.

Let me conclude this chapter with a look at the state of the retired, amongst the majority of whom there is little or no work, little or no purposeful activity. The state of the retired is especially important at present because of the general agreement that earlier retirement on as considerable a scale as is financially possible is one of the ways of tackling the problem of mass unemployment. There is an assumption that the retired (on pension) will live more happily than the unemployed live on social security. Therefore, it is suggested, let us retire people early and give their jobs to the unemployed. In so far as the aged are infirm, early retirement is obviously a blessing. On the other hand, for the fit and partially fit, life in retirement can be most unsatisfying. If we are to retire people at fifty-five (or earlier) the prospect of rest and relaxation and time for the garden (if there is one) may be enticing. In fact, it often does not work out that way at all; nothing to do may be very frustrating; time and energy may be hopelessly wasted in enforced inactivity. Some of the retired die quite quickly. A discerning Toronto doctor told me of his surprise at the death within a year of retirement of a friend who appeared to be perfectly fit before he retired. I was myself interested in Queensland when relatively young graziers gave up their hard work in the bush to live in considerable luxury in retirement on the Queensland Gold Coast. Many of them lived for very few years.

Some people indeed die mentally long before they die physically. The retired may continue to feel wanted, but are conscious of being of little use to anyone. David Dunning, of Ripon College, Cuddesdon (at the time of his writing) has done some useful research and writing concerning the problems of the aged (and the not so aged) in Oxfordshire.[27] He says that 'elderlyness is a quite inadequate word with which to describe the retired'. It disguises the complexity of life-styles, vocations, behaviour, relationships and expectations. He claims that 'the seemingly endless amount of time at one's disposal', the lack of responsibility for earning a living, and the lack of ability to promote one's standard of living are burdens which may lead to decline. He writes of the unsatisfactory nature of much of the kindly work of ministering to the aged. Luncheon clubs, he says, are no solution to real problems. All the vast energy put by others into cooking, fetching, carrying, providing, entertaining and organizing leaves the elderly themselves merely to sit and eat. They need, so far as they have the capacity, to do things for themselves. Dunning goes on to make suggestions for alleviating the unhappiness of unoccupied retirement. It is purposive activity which they need, work itself according to this book's definition of the word. On 27 February 1983 an appeal was made on the radio for the Employment Fellowship. Among other activities, one of the functions of this organization is to help the retired to find and do work which is within their capacity (and which does not compete with the work of those not retired). The need, we were told, is very great.

I have tried to make it plain that man does not necessarily need paid employment, but that he does require work (according again to my definition of the word), so long as he has any capacity for activity in him. Miss X retired recently from her isolated home in the Welsh hills to an Oxfordshire old people's home. She dealt bravely with the transition, only saying quietly that she could not and would not sit around doing nothing for the rest of her life. She was at work in the garden and (for hours) in the kitchen within a few days of her arrival. Mr Smith (shall we call him?) retired at sixty only in order that he might take another job. Now he has retired from that other job, and is busier than ever. He has just returned from a trip to Nepal. Mr Peter Prior of Bulmers Cider (when I saw him last) was looking forward to compulsory retirement at 62. He anticipated with relish the new work which he intended to take up. My old pupil Niel is in his mid-sixties. He would very much like to go to the University when he retires, to read for a degree. 'Mrs Windmill' is just eighty, and is seriously crippled with arthritis. She knits and knits and knits. She says that she 'always likes to be making something'. She keeps remarkably young. A much older lady has difficulty both in moving and in seeing, but declares that she likes to have something to do. She does cross-stitch in wool on binca cloth. The result is very pleasing. She first won a prize for this sort of work when she was seven years old. That was quite a time ago; she is in her early nineties now. May is not so old. She worked for two years at millinery at Bourne and Hollingsworth's and for fifty years at fancy millinery at Marshall and Snelgrove's. She is still doing a good day's work for the nuns in a conventual embroidery room. Sister X is considerably older. She says that she always has a needle in her hand. Sister Y has her health problems. The Sisters are most anxious to spare her exertion, to stop her from running to the door and going to the post. She does not in the least want to be stopped. Only recently after a long life of service she has discovered a new mode of service with 'her men' who come for food at the Convent door. She sits by the Convent door and knits while she waits for them. Sister Z is not so old as some, but her heart is not very strong. Apart from her Office and the Eucharist, she makes exquisite children's toys: monkeys, donkeys, elephants, penguins, ducks, in all sorts of gorgeous colours. I tackled her concerning the significance of this work of hers. She just said, 'Without it, I would peg out'. She seems sometimes when she is on telephone duty to be doing three or four jobs at once. Two other (non-conventual) elderly ladies tell me in all seriousness that they would not know what to do with themselves without work. It is this, they say, that really keeps them alive. All these older persons are typical in their realization of their need to keep working, representative of the whole human need to work.

The writing of Viktor Frankl, an Austrian psychiatrist who became a prisoner in a Nazi concentration camp (Auschwitz), is relevant. He declared, à propos of the large number of prisoners who decayed and died in the camp:

> The prisoner who had lost faith in the future was doomed. With his loss of belief in the future, . . . he let himself decline and became subject to mental and physical decay. . . . Those who know how close the connection is between the state of mind of a man . . . and the state of immunity of his body will understand that the sudden loss of hope and courage can have a deadly effect.

He frequently quoted Nietzsche who said, 'He who has a *why* to live can bear with almost any *how*'. Yet it is not enough for a retired person to have the hope of a game of bowls for Saturday. He must have the hope of something more fundamental to him, the hope of being someone, doing something that matters to someone outside himself, something that counts, the hope of a life of some sort of purposeful activity. Frankl watched with the trained eye of the psychiatrist the reactions of his fellow prisoners to appalling privations. Those who became unable to work were sent to the death chambers. He makes it clear that 'those who did come through were not the physically more robust but those who were buoyed up by hope'. Persons tending towards despair had to learn, he wrote, that what mattered was 'what life expects from us'. He said that life meant 'taking the responsibility . . . to fulfil the tasks which it constantly sets for each individual'.[28] Those who satisfactorily survive the early retirement of the non-infirm will be those who are buoyed up by the reasoned hope of having something to do the next day. Those who have no hope of having anything to do worth doing begin to die. People with reasoned hope fight for life, people without it put up little fight.

Alistair Cooke, the distinguished commentator on American affairs, tenders advice over the radio to those in danger of retirement: 'If you're old enough to retire, and are about to do so, don't do it. Men, especially men, who retire, keel over or they go hard in the head and become a nuisance in the house'. That is a very relevant point. The CBI rejected in 1982 the advice of its annual (1981) conference to support earlier retirement. It must have realized that it is humanly dangerous to have nothing to do. All that Cooke says, all that I have tried to say, concerning the danger of too early retirement applies tragically to the unemployed. To be deprived of work, of purposeful activity, of the opportunity in some measure to change the environment, is dehumanizing, killing, the beginning of the end. As the London representative of *The Washington Post* said on BBC radio on 16 August 1982: 'It is better for a man to work hard than to tend the traditional roses.' The unemployed person tends to lose hope. He cannot even be bothered to trim the roses. The community tends to blame him for that. But the community must begin to accept some responsibility for his unemployment, some responsibility for giving him work.

NOTES

1 Lutterworth, p. 396

2 *Theology of Work*, a paper delivered at St. George's House, Windsor, 1977.

3 M. Austin et P. Vidal-Naquet: *Economies et Sociétés en Grèce Ancienne*, Armand Colin, Paris, 1972, pp. 27-8.

4 *Rhetoric*, I, 9, 1367a, 30.

5 *Politics*, I, 4, 1254a, 6.

6 *Op.Cit.*, p. 28.

7 H. D. F. Kitto: *The Greeks*, Penguin, 1951, p. 246.

8 ibid., p. 100.

9 ibid., p. 241.

10 ibid., p. 243.

11 *Politics* I, 2, 1253a, I.

12 *The Greeks (op.cit.)*, p. 244.

13 F. Finley: *The Ancient Economy*, Chatto and Windus, 1979, p. 82 (1st published 1973).

14 ibid., p. 68.

15 ibid., p. 71.

16 ibid., p. 80.

17 *The Greeks (op.cit.)*, pp. 131-2, 134.

18 *The Greek Commonwealth*, Clarendon Press, 1922, p. 272 (1st published 1915).

19 ibid., p. 259.

20 ibid., p. 395.

21 G. Glotz: *Le Travail dans la Grèce Ancienne*, Félix Ancan, Paris, 1920, p. 198.

22 R. B. Hassrick: *North American Indians*, p. 20.

23 Toronto *Globe and Mail*, 6 July 1982, p. 16.

24 *Gypsy Politics and Change*, Routledge and Kegan Paul, 1974, pp. 64, 54.

25 *Oxford Star*, 15/16 July, p. 6.

26 *Gypsy Politics (op.cit.)*, p. 3.

27 *How are the Elderly getting on in Oxfordshire?*, 1981.

28 *Man's Search for Meaning*, Simon & Schuster, New York, 1962, pp. 74-5, XI, 77 (1st published 1946).

In what I have written concerning the gypsies I have been greatly helped by Fr. Eltin Daly, ofm.cap.

5

Theologizing about Work and Unemployment

In the development of what is intended to be a reasoned argument against the toleration of unemployment, on the ground that human beings need work in order to be persons, I have tried to explain something of the psychology and philosophy of work. Once again, I repeat that by 'work' I am not merely referring to paid employment. Persons require work in order to become truly human and are damaged if work is not available. However, behind nature, including human nature, the Christian believes that there is God. Let us try now to see if our limited knowledge of God, our ideas about God, can throw any light upon human nature and work and unemployment. I am seeking not only for what helps us to understand man and his work but for what may inspire at least the theist and the Christian to take more seriously the human tragedy of the deprivation of work. One more recitation of the cruel facts and figures of unemployment, with appropriate stories to illustrate them, may seem only repetitive and sentimental to many who have read the like before. However, if one can in some measure show that unemployment is contrary to the will of God, some may be aroused to the necessary hard thought and steely will towards remedial action.

One source of our knowledge of God, according to Christians, is the Bible. Very early in the first book of the Bible we find a conception of man 'made in the image of God'. In *Genesis* 1, 26-7, we are told that God said, 'Let us make man in our image and likeness to rule the fish in the sea, the birds of heaven, the cattle, all wild animals on earth, and all reptiles that crawl upon the earth'. The priestly writer goes on: 'So God created man in his own image; in the image of God he created him.'[1] This is often interpreted to mean that the creative God made man to be creative like him. *Genesis* continues: 'God . . . said to them, be fruitful and increase, fill the earth and subdue it.' Pope John Paul II in his 1981 *Laborem Exercens* (the *Encyclical Letter on Human Work*) refers to this description of the creation of man as 'the first gospel of work'.[2] The late Dean Alan Richardson believed that the *Genesis* stories really do provide a basis for a Christian doctrine of work. He quoted *Genesis* 2, 15: 'The Lord God took the man and put him in the Garden of Eden to till it and care for it'. He went on to say à propos of these *Genesis* myths that 'work is a necessity for man, . . . it is man's proper nature to be a worker'.[3] The texts, however, are isolated, no part of any great biblical theme. It is recognised by many now that isolated texts are inadequate bases for great Christian doctrines. These *Genesis* texts belong to those collections of ancient stories which abounded in Palestine and the countries to the north and east of it, 'raw bits and pieces of myth, legend, saga and what not', as Bruce Vawter describes them. The same scholar goes on: 'As raw materials they are almost entirely and without exception identifiable in terms of the literary and thought-forms common to the ancient near-Eastern culture of which *Genesis* and Israel were a tiny part.'[4] They may well testify primarily to the current belief that God was man-like, rather than to the later belief of those who incorporated these stories in *Genesis*, that man was God-like. Gerhard von Rad writes that the texts cannot be expounded 'without ambiguity', that to be made 'in the image of God' simply means that man resembles God.[5] We really cannot theologize too seriously on these texts.

There is also to be considered the myth in *Genesis* 3, 16-19, which suggests that work is punishment for disobedience to God:

> To the woman he said: 'I will increase your labour and your groaning, and in labour you shall bear children. . . . And it to the man he said: 'Because you have listened to your wife and have eaten from the tree which I forbade you, accursed shall be the ground on your account. With labour you shall win your food from it all the days of your life. It will grow thorns and thistles for you, none but wild plants for you to eat. You shall gain your bread by the sweat of your brow'.

The late Dr J. A. C. Brown, one-time Director of the Institute of Social Psychiatry in London, is gratefully remembered by ex-servicemen for his wise guidance to many of them who served in the Middle East in the 1939-45 War. Yet his uncritical acceptance as 'the orthodox view of work' of the *Genesis* story that 'physical labour is a curse imposed on man as a punishment for his sins'[6] has surprised many and convinced few. Dr Brown himself refuted this allegedly 'orthodox view'. Only the old-fashioned or the biblical fundamentalist would wish to spend time upon a doctrine of work founded upon such a text.

Despite valiant Roman Catholic attempts to create one during the last ninety years, there is perhaps no 'orthodox view' of the connection between God and man's work. However, the present Pope, John Paul II, is following in the footsteps of his recent predecessors in trying to create one. In *Laborem Exercens* he uses many biblical texts and demonstrates a good deal of human wisdom as well. Here is a papal letter written far more clearly and more nearly in contemporary language than has been the case in previous Encyclicals. A distinguished Roman Catholic scholar writes to me of it, 'It's really quite a positive document, even if it is far too wordy and repetitive'. Like all papal pronouncements it still needs to some extent to be simplified and translated. On page 59 of *Laborem Exercens* the Pope begins to expound his biblically-based doctrine of work. 'Man must work', he writes, 'because the Creator has commanded it.' He quotes the Second Vatican Council concerning human work: 'To believers, this point is settled . . . such human activity accords with God's will. For man, created to God's image, received a mandate to subject to himself the earth and all that it contains . . .'[7] This refers to *Genesis* 1, 28. The ecologist does not care much for this conception of 'subduing' the earth. However, that does not bother the Pope. He goes on to show that the Bible as a whole seems to endorse this teaching of man's work as God's will. He notes that the Ten Commandments which require a rest for man every seventh day confirm God's will for man to work on the other days.[8] The Pope goes on to quote Old and New Testament examples of man's different sorts of work, as if the Word of God were thereby implicitly sanctioning them. He writes of Jesus's many references, with seeming approval, to human work.[9] He commends St Paul's obvious pride in his trade and in his ability to earn his own living. The Pope notes St Paul's condemnation of idleness and his exhortation to his readers to 'work heartily, as serving the Lord and not man' (*Colossians* 3, 23).[10]

We have heard this kind of thing before and are surely morally at one with St Paul and the Pope. If the question of human work has been 'a constant factor . . . of the Church's teaching',[11] as the Pope says, that teaching seems to have been more obvious in the Protestant Work Ethic than in the popular orthodoxy of the Roman Catholic Church. However, we must in no sense denigrate the significance of such modern papal teaching as that of *Rerum*

Novarum of Leo XIII (of 1891).[12] The ninetieth anniversary of this Encyclical provoked this most carefully prepared (and revised after the Pope's shooting) *Laborem Exercens* of Pope John Paul II. As a 'Young Christian Worker' said to me: 'It is surprising and pleasing that the Pope is interested in work at all.' The Pope declares that for 'almost a hundred years' since the publication of *Rerum Novarum,* the Church has been directing her teaching 'and the many undertakings connected with her apostolic mission' to the social question. At the centre of this, he says, is work.[13] One feels that Christians have not quite received this message or at any rate have failed to absorb it. Members of the Church, Christians as a whole, do not seem to have grasped that work is at the heart of the social question. Nor have they really understood that gospel and faith have something to say about it. There have been few stirrings of conscience, few voices on either side of industry to represent Christian concern. Certainly in Britain there has been inadequate representation of Christian teaching on work. Whatever the Popes (or the Lambeth Conferences for that matter) may have said about work (and unemployment) during the last hundred years, both the ordinary churchman and the man in the street tend to think that the Church is primarily interested in spiritual matters and in man's future rather than in his present work (or his lack of it).

In *Laborem Exercens* we see a brave and dedicated Pope trying to arouse in his flock and in all his fellow-Christians a care for the worker and compassion for the person deprived of work. Because of the value of work to man, the human value of it, he realizes and draws attention to the human impoverishment caused by unemployment. He calls unemployment 'the opposite of a just and right situation'; he says that it is 'in all cases' an evil. This is strong language. When unemployment reaches a certain level, he says, 'it . . . can become a real social disaster'. He writes of the need for 'overall planning' to 'meet the danger of unemployment and to ensure employment for all'.[14] From biblical texts and from human insights he gives us teaching that is relevant and wise. Yet *Laborem Exercens* does not seem to have made a deep and lasting impression upon its readers and his Church. It looks as if there has to be some other form of presentation of such teaching, a new drawing upon human experience if human beings are to hear and learn. I am thinking of that kind of human experience which is called 'grass roots theology' and which I shall explain shortly. Dr C. H. Whiteley, formerly Reader in Philosophy at the University of Birmingham, wrote (with his wife) of what they believed concerning the human impact of such ecclesiastical pronouncements as the Pope's: 'During a long experience of ethical discussion with university students and a variety of adult education classes, while we have met people (mostly Catholics) who based their morality on ecclesiastical authority, we have found scarcely anyone who tried to settle a disputed point by . . . quoting the Bible.'[15] There are many Roman Catholics (and others) who would agree.

It seems to be a fact that, at any rate in this age, pronouncements from on high concerning faith are not very effective, even when scripturally authenticated. Papal encyclicals are not rejected; they are received and not acted on. They are examples of a 'theology from above'. Ordinary people, including many Church people, do not consider them relevant to their lives, however many texts they may employ. To many people such pronouncements sometimes do not sound as if they correlate with human experience. No chord is struck; there is no favourable human response when they are heard. All know how true this is, for example, when the Pope condemns contraception. A large proportion of his own people, who are well aware of his views, continue to practise it. There is a large collection of 'guaranteed', authoritative sets of propositions from the Bible, the Creeds and the official ecclesiastical dogmas; this collection has been called 'Denziger theology'. It is so named after a volume of quotations from Councils and Popes on dogmatic questions first made by Henry Denziger in 1854. 'The logic of such a theology is that "Denziger" consists of a collection of true theological statements with reference to which any theological utterance may be checked. This is an extreme form of the use of some notion of primarily propositional truth in theology. . . . Its characteristic is a search for propositions that enshrine the truth.'[16] However significant, however true indeed this 'theology from above' may possibly be, much of it leaves the majority of ordinary people, including Roman Catholics, unimpressed. People tend to form their own convictions, based to some extent at least upon their own experience of life and (as they may think) of God. I have had a distinguished ecclesiastic recently staying in my house. A young scientist who had been feeling his way towards God in various local places of worship came to see him. He wanted to ask him (and did ask him) why he believed in God. The Church with its worship and doctrine had failed to convince him; he was prepared to be convinced by the experience and witness of one individual whom he respected.

I am seeking for theological sanction for a doctrine of work as the satisfaction of an urge for purposeful activity of social significance. I have not found satisfying authority in the scripture-based teaching of the Pope. I seek to arouse people to a refusal to tolerate mass unemployment, and do not find that they are so aroused as a result of official Church teaching. Yet there need be no prejudice against 'theology from above' if it is realized and admitted that such teaching has within it an inevitable human element. The distinguished Flemish theologian Edward Schillebeeckx writes of the inadequacy of our 'authoritative' talk of God. He tells us that 'revealed truth' depends upon the human experience which receives it. There is no revelation, he says, without experience.[17] He writes that revelation is 'an interpretative experience'.[18] He is helping the Church to help the world to see that 'official' theology has its human limitations. Here at last is something which the ordinary worker can begin to understand: a sense of man humbly but diligently seeking after the truth of God. The ordinary worker is sensitive to that, sympathetic with the seeking. Canon Leslie Houlden, of King's College, London, goes along with Schillebeeckx. He writes that with reference to 'the truth about God and from God', a 'last word' from us must always be 'blasphemous in principle, idolatrous in practice'.[19] Schillebeeckx explains: 'We get only a limited perspective on the transcending God via his immanence and traces in this world, in history and in man, in our fellow-man.' 'Indeed,' he writes, 'there is for us only a "seeing the back of God", as the Old Testament puts it.'[20] He sums up: 'Critical knowledge of our ignorance does not give up the will for truth, but rejects any absolute knowledge. It has the courage to express the inexpressible clumsily, knowing that this comes nearer to reality than dumb silence or the dogmatic attitude.'[21]

In the theology of work (and unemployment), a seeking for theological meaning and for theological insight ought to go on, in the Church as a whole, as with the individual. The will for truth ought to go forward, because man's very salvation is at stake. Man is concerned deep down within himself with what he ought to be, with what he ought to do. Deep down within him, unemployment is an outrage to him, and he must seek to try to understand why it is an outrage. There may develop vaguely in him a grass roots theology, a sense that this outrage imposed upon him is against the nature of things, against the order of the universe. He may be at least prepared to consider that this is the concern of a personal God. Mrs Ursula King, of Leeds University, writes most interestingly: 'Today we are experiencing a deep transformation of religious awareness, often taking place at the margin or outside the official religious institutions . . . The model of how to do theology is changing from a deductive to an inductive approach, based on human experience here and now.'[22] A worker for the South London Industrial Mission, at the end of his first year with the Mission wrote:

> Above all, I value the stress that was placed on the inductive approach to theology, in that it is not an academic subject to be studied and learnt about in universities, but something that you hammer out on the shop floor. We are encouraged to start with real life situations that confront us, seek to relate our convictions to the situation and see what practical implications for action this process requires.
>
> I feel that I have been given the clue to a method that is capable of considerable development.[23]

'The theologian', writes Leslie Houlden, 'must listen not only to the official church, with its inevitable and in part proper conservatism, but to the world at large. . . . The theologian must try out his words . . . but always subject to Christian experience.'[24] The SLIM Missioner is right in sensing that the theology from 'real life' may influence life more than 'theology from above'.

Let us do a little 'theologizing from below' concerning work. Let us see if man has any 'sense' from within or around himself of work as God's will for man (as the Pope regards it) and of what the Pope means when he calls unemployment 'in all cases . . . an evil'. Does the worker, do workers in general, have any conception of God's will for them to fulfil themselves in their work? Some of us may remember seeing on our television screens in January 1982 scenes of the wide-spread flooding of the river Ouse as a result of heavy snowfalls. Streets and ground floors of houses were under water in parts of the York-Selby area of Yorkshire. In the midst of such local and domestic disasters, people left their snow-bound homes, sometimes even left the upper storey rooms of their flooded houses, in order that (by Land-Rover or by boat), they might get into the cities and towns to do their work, to get to their jobs. They were mostly people who really wanted to clean up their own homes, to stay at home to prepare for worse; yet off they went somehow to their ordinary jobs for the day. It was not the fear of losing their monetary rewards which drove them to their work. It was a sense of the rightness of going to work, an unspoken, a subconscious knowledge of a genuine vocation. It was to be seen again on Wednesday, 10 March 1982. There was no public transport in London that day in protest against the suppression of the Greater London Council's 'cheap fares' policy. Over the London bridges in their thousands poured in on foot the workers from the suburbs, in some cases walking many miles to work. There was a sense of moral imperative that this was right, that this had to be done. 'Taking the day off', justifiable though it may have been, would have meant for those workers being untrue to themselves. There is, we are told 'from above', a transcendent God who creates man 'in his own image', to be creative, to 'till' and to 'care'. Here amongst these people getting themselves to work somehow under difficulties was something 'from below' in man: a sense that this ought to be done. If it was not a theology, it was at least a moral foundation on which a grass roots theology could be built.

The majority of these people could not say where this 'voice from within' came from. It would be fair enough if they claimed it to be the voice of conscience. The Christian would go further. He would say that it was indeed the voice of conscience, a reflection of the 'inner', 'unconscious' mind of man under the influence of the Spirit of God. So long as conscience is at work, persons will be uneasy if they do not work, however much they may pretend to the contrary. Conscience concerning work usually (not always) reflects the will of God. Let people be careful of accusing the 'layabouts' of having no conscience concerning the obtaining of work. Repeated failure breeds sometimes in the unemployed a stance, a façade of not caring. Deep down within himself the unemployed person cares terribly. It is not a question of 'the will of God for him' at the present time. It is a question of what he was made for, what he exists for. Certainly, it was not for the misery and humiliation of unemployment. On the other hand, as we shall see in the next chapter, unemployment often leads, especially if prolonged, to a sickness of the mind, a loss of self-confidence. There is sometimes more than a sickness; there is a rotting, a loss of even the will to work.

In its appeal to man, in its seeking to help him, the Church would often do better to persuade him to look within himself, to try to understand what is happening there than to quote scripture or encyclicals. In the past, Anglicans learned the Catechism of the *Book of Common Prayer*. In that Catechism the Anglican child was taught 'to do my duty in that state of life, unto which it shall please God to call me'. Rightly this is no longer learnt; for it might suggest that the poor man was destined by God to remain permanently at the rich man's gate. Yet this 'theology from above' reflected rather than inspired that 'theology from below' which leads many to believe that they ought to work, and some to believe that this is how they were made by God. 'I shall go crazy', said my Iranian friend yesterday, 'if I don't get work'. Many 'feel in their bones' that mass unemployment is against God's will but do not know what to do about it. They need, we need, to let this truth work on within us, until we burn with the sense that we must all do something to rid the community of the scourge of unemployment. I shall suggest in the last chapter ways which may very well involve self-sacrifice.

Some shared in 1982 in the agony of (the now deceased) Bert in ITV's *Coronation Street*, when he lost his job. We came to life again with him when at last he acquired a job as a fitter. In the past, men were happy to take their family names from the job they did. Hence the Bakers, the Smiths, the Butchers, the Watermans, even the Smithsons. Today some relic of this remains. I ask John what he is, and he tells me that he is a fishmonger. I ask 'Mary' what she is, and she tells me that she is a housewife. Forgetting that he is unemployed, I foolishly ask Peter what he is. He replies, quite cheerfully, 'I'm nothing'. He has nothing to call himself by; he has no identity; he is 'out of work'. 'Jane' echoes him. She says: 'I am neither typist nor wife nor mother. I have nothing to do and I do not know what to call myself.' If what a person calls himself is so important to him that he replies to the question concerning what he is by telling you what he does, work must signify a great deal to man. And 'to be nothing' is a very serious state of being. It is, in fact, a state of non-being. 'God help me, if they take my gifts from me,' writes the young woman on the verge of unemployment.

Man intuitively believes in the 'rightness' of work, whatever he may have to say against it. He is depressed, sometimes to the point of suicide, sometimes to that of vandalism or of rioting, when he finds himself out of work. It is not true that a job is merely a matter of status, of what the neighbours think. It is a matter of self-respect. He knows what is due from himself to society; he must work. He knows deep down within himself what is due to him from society: a chance to work. He is dismayed, and his sense of the rightness of things is damaged, when he finds himself unemployed, apparently un-needed. He who, according to the Christian doctrine of creation, has been made by God, knows that he too must somehow, in some measure, be creative, that he ought to be able to feel that he is somehow altering the environment. As we have seen before, to do so only in his own home or back garden is not good enough for one who is essentially a social being.

Professor David Donnison, former chairman of the Supplementary Benefits Commission, tells us of some of the unemployed that:

> If no other ingredient is added to the brew, these excluded people simply grow depressed. They may drink too much, quarrel with their wives, fall ill or commit suicide . . . but they do not come out onto the streets. They sit at home instead, listlessly watching television.

However, he goes on to say that where there are concentrations of young unemployed people, especially where people in the parental age groups are thin on the ground, where the property is decrepit and over-crowded, but discos and pubs and clubs bring them together, the flashpoint for rioting is close at hand. He goes on:

> The climate which makes riots a possibility pervades cities in which large numbers of people are excluded, without hope of better things to come, from a regular job, good wages, and opportunities for getting married and settling down to raise a family in a decent home. Poverty, frustration and

humiliation are their daily experience, now and for the foreseeable future. They have been castrated.

He concludes:

> They all pay the price of the economic mismanagement, the social neglect and the injustices rife in a society which stunts so many human hopes and talents. We cannot put an end to violence on the streets unless we tackle these fundamental problems.[25]

Unemployment is inhuman and ungodly. The living God, whose image is Jesus, did not make man for this. That image of God was himself a carpenter. We do not need an encyclical to tell us all this. The ordinary person who is inclined to believe in 'some sort of God somewhere' knows most of this. Let the Church of God in the name of the people of God say loudly and clearly that to do nothing much about unemployment when there is much to be done (at a cost) is against the will of God. From the grass roots all around it will come back an echo of this theology: 'That is right, that is true'. Government has been frightened into doing a little by rioting in Brixton and Toxteth and elsewhere. It would be better for Church and nation if the Church were to warn very loudly and clearly that where there is no work, there will in course of time surely be violence. There must be in and from man purposeful activity of social significance. Whether it be constructive or destructive, there is in man a will to alter the environment.

I have spoken of the will of God for man. Sometimes this is recognized and acknowledged. Sometimes persons think only in terms of a conscience which recognizes an obligation to do what is just and right. There is very little atheism; but there are various factors which contribute to an intellectual sloth, a failure even to look behind the moral imperative, to seek to see if some power, some personal influence is at work. There is, on the other hand, an openness to the idea of God amongst workers who could not proclaim themselves Christian. I have been on shop floors in the north and the west and the east, and have been amazed at the friendliness and the sense of fellow-feeling that has come over to me from workers. There has been an obvious sense that we are on the same side. This has been quite unexpected. I do not think it has been fanciful. Only once have I been asked, quite pleasantly, what I thought I was doing 'out of my parish, and on a shop floor'. The question was asked with interest rather than resentment. I have stayed recently, in both cases for several days, with two groups of trade unionists, the first a small one of relatively young men, chiefly electricians, and the other a much larger one of mostly middle-aged miners. In both cases, my initial shyness and diffidence have been met by an attitude that assumed a basic oneness of mind.

How much real 'basic oneness of mind'? I have tried to check on this with members of these groups and with others, all hourly paid workers, some shop stewards. Alan, a young convener, who does not go to church but sends his two children to a Church school, is sure that his mates do believe in a God who creates man for a purpose. In his former job in a small workshop, they 'used to talk together about such things'. Now, in a big shop, with only a half-hour dinner break, the opportunities do not arise. He says: 'Take death. When a person dies young, people are shocked. He was meant to live a whole life, do something in life. People ask "Why?" But they all want a religious service.' They are puzzled, Alan is saying: their deep-seated belief in a purpose for man is outraged; yet their basic 'faith' does not lead them to reject God.

'Jack' is a middle-aged Roman Catholic shop steward. He believes that man is 'meant to be' a worker. He has no doubt about that. He is 'sure' that 'all workers' believe in a creative God. However, he is inclined to think that only shop stewards realize that man was created for a purpose. He says this because it is only shop stewards, he says, who understand responsibility, understand what work is all about. It is not that he is conceited. He just feels that industry has not helped workers (as it might have done) to think about their work. A shop steward cannot help but think, he says. When he thinks, in comes God. This is not, of course, he agrees, limited to Roman Catholics. That is what Jack thinks anyhow. 'Ted' is a rather older man. His experience as an electrician is wide and varied. I shall quote him in a later chapter concerning his opinion of the microprocessor. He does not think that being a shop steward makes any difference to your belief in and about God. He says that the question of God is an on-going one in your life. 'I'm always looking and thinking,' he says. 'Is it true or isn't it? Do I believe or don't I?' he asks himself. He comes down on the whole on the side of belief. He says that to him it is important that his children go to a Church school. 'They must have the opportunity to believe,' he says. He is convinced that the way you live depends on what you believe. He believes you ought to help; he would never pass a stranded motorist on the road without trying to help. He believes in helping at work. He believes in working hard if need be. He only asks that management tell him what is happening, why the thing needs doing in this way and needs doing now. He reckons that we are supposed to be unselfish. 'After all,' he says, 'other people do exist.' Basically, he says that he knows in his heart, or he thinks that he knows, that 'God and unselfishness and helpfulness are all bound up together'. Those are his words. He says that if you want peace, you will find it in a church (even he says, in a little mortuary chapel where you happen to be doing some wiring). However, he does not go to church very often. He believes that most people think like him. He says, echoing Alan, that people think a lot when trouble hits them. Perhaps, he says, God is testing them out. He could go along with that. He does not normally air his opinions; when he does, he is blunt, frank and (I believe) immensely honest.

Prince Charles some years ago, in an off-the-cuff interview with an American journalist, did a little grass-roots theologizing. He said (without making a sentence of it): 'Surely, the reason, I think, for our existence on this earth: to try and make the most of our human qualities and our human adaptability.' I do not think he learned this from the Archbishop of Canterbury or from the chaplain at Gordonstoun School. Ted is right. There is a good deal of quiet theologizing among non-theologically-orientated persons. Sometimes there is the will to do what seems to be right, at whatever cost. In the last chapter I shall suggest that in the fight against unemployment the nation will require people prepared to make sacrifices. It may be that the people whom the nation needs will be the minority who, consciously or unconsciously, have grasped something of the divine order, of the divine will, who may even have some conception of God's kingdom and of that kingdom's law of love for one's neighbour, which makes the toleration of unemployment impossible.

In seeking for signs of recognition of God in man, one may well have to be content with recognition only of his attributes, of the signs of his presence. There is a grass roots theology which speaks only of the things of God, but which implies his being. Columbus had to learn that the world was round before he could discover the West Indies. I remember talking at St Mark's College, Townsville, to a tall young student whom years ago I had taught as a small boy in a Mount Isa State School. Now he was trying with all his strength to make me understand that for him God came over in the words and sounds of pop music. 'Can't you see . . .?' he said to me. I had not seen at all; it had not crossed my mind; but now I could begin to see. For many the beginning of finding God will be the finding of oneself in freedom. The lad was finding in himself through pop music that God whom I myself had failed to reveal to him as a child with my 'theology from above'.

When years ago with the (Anglican) Christian Workers Union I tried to inculcate the idea amongst young folk that work was primarily for God, that 'God was the ultimate master', I scored no outstanding success. Far from it. A (Roman Catholic) Young Christian Worker gave me the obvious answer very recently. 'I don't work for God,' she said, 'I work for Mr Jones.' It may be that for young workers the best we can hope for, if it can be achieved, is that sense that in their work they find themselves, express themselves and enjoy fellowship. This, we may say, is what God wants for them now. In the course of their self-development, as they begin to think what they are doing and what it is all about, they may become aware of one who is behind everything and who has a purpose for them.

The uninhibited self-development of the young worker sometime results in real experience of God. Pope John XXIII was drawing on theology from below rather than on theology from above when he wrote in *Mater et Magistra* (1961): 'In the work on the farm the human personality finds every incentive for self-expression, self-development and spiritual growth.'[26] In finding and fulfilling himself he tends to move towards God. Gerard Manley Hopkins, the Jesuit poet, wrote of a person's self-development, comparing it to a bell 'flinging out broad its name':

Each mortal thing does one thing and the same:
Deals out that being indoors each one dwells;
Selves-goes itself; *myself* it speaks and spells;
Crying *What I do is me: for that I came*.[27]

From experience of satisfying working life can emerge theology, experience of, knowledge of God. Tillich, the Protestant theologian, wrote that 'the object of theology is what concerns us ultimately'. He went on to say that 'only these statements are theological which deal with their object in so far as it can become a matter of being or non-being for us'. 'Nothing', he said, 'can be of ultimate concern for us which does not have the power of threatening and saving our being'.[28] The unemployed tend to have no 'ultimate concern'. They are weighed down, their minds anchored to the loneliness and misery of the present. I asked young Nicky a couple of days ago if he had ever had a job. He said 'No'. It is 1985, and he is twenty-one. People complain about him. He is what society has made him. I should not expect him to have any thought of God.

I have met in the Soviet Union young working persons who laughed at the very idea of God. Yet older working persons there did not appear to dismiss the idea of God so casually. At any rate, I am trying to say that there are depths within the human mind which are by no means visible on the television screen. Here various kinds of thoughts moving towards reality find a home. A man in very early middle age, with great experience of a variety of mankind, said to me recently that he believed with heart and soul in 'the rightness' (as he put it) of the mind of the ordinary working person. Certainly work, fulfilling as it is, helps that mind to develop. Most Christians, Catholic and Protestant, realize the fundamental human importance of work, whether it leads a person to conscious experience of God or not. The World Council of Churches in 1948 declared that the Christian Church has an urgent responsibility to help man to achieve a fuller personal life within the technical society.[29] The Second Vatican Council declared of God and man:

> Human activity proceeds from man: it is also ordered to him. When he works, not only does he transform matter and society, but he fulfils himself. . . . Rightly understood, this kind of growth is more precious than any kind of wealth that can be amassed. It is what a man is, rather than what he has, that counts. . . . Here then is the norm for human activity . . . to harmonize with the authentic interests of the human race, in accordance with God's will and design, and to enable men as individuals and as members of society to pursue and fulfil their total vocation.

The Council went on to speak of 'every man's duty to work . . . as well as his right to work'. It said: 'It is the duty of society to see to it that, according to the prevailing circumstances, all citizens have the opportunity of finding employment.'[30] In speaking thus, Vatican II quotes no texts from scripture. It refers to encyclicals, papal 'messages' and 'allocutions'. It is in fact referring chiefly to these insights which have risen up within the Church rather than to that theology from above which we normally call divine revelation. This kind of teaching which has grown within the Church during the past ninety years is in fact the continuing development of those insights into the significance of man and his work which were first publicly exhibited in the *Rerum Novarum* of Leo XIII in 1891. Sociology is affecting theology, and new growth in the latter is coming up from human soil. Popes and Councils are learning from human experience. This does not cast doubt on the truth of the fruits of that experience. On the other hand, it does commend those fruits to the many people of today who greatly value what arises from genuine human experience.

For those Christians who also greatly value divine revelation, theology from above, it is comforting to study Edward Schillebeeckx. He makes it clear that there is in fact no fundamental distinction between theology from above and theology from below. In the formulation of both, man is always at work; in the formulation of both, God is sometimes at work. 'The New Testament', writes Schillebeeckx, 'bubbling over with praise for "blessings from above", does not know the later contrast between what comes "from below" and what comes "from above".'[31] He tells us that 'we know God's revelations only in the form of human ideas and words about divine revelation'.[32] He tells us that 'reality is always more than and different from what we imagine it to be'.[33] He says that 'the inadequacy of our talk of God is no reason for silence'.[34]

Schillebeeckx, therefore, reinforces faith in theology from below, in grass roots theology, in the validity of the search for and feeling after God in the midst of human experience. He declares that God reveals himself in revealing man to himself.[35] He writes in a fascinating way of our 'faith language about God' having 'an experiential basis . . . in our human situation within the world and history'. He explains that 'our speaking about God's transcendence has no ground other than our own contingency'.[36] He says that 'when therefore we consider God, it can only be from within the perspective provided by the non-divine, that is, by precisely what does not make God God'.[37] He pictures salvation as a growing process towards that unity with Christ in which it is completed. Working man, growing in personal fulfilment, is growing also, whether he knows it or not, towards saving knowledge and experience of Christ. The corollary of this for the unemployed we shall study shortly.

Schillebeeckx defines salvation as 'well-being', 'haleness, being whole', 'saving health', 'final good'. 'Salvation', he says, 'is for the healing and making whole of each'.[38] He writes:

> Salvation . . . finds expression in the full sense of the word as perfect and universal salvation or wholeness for each and every individual, for man as a person, as a physical being, as a fellow man, and also for man as he is called to create liberating structures and institutions, for man as homo faber, as homo ludens, as homo oeconomicus, as homo contemplativus, above all as man who longs for justice and love; salvation, finally, for all men, in present, past and future, living or dead.[39]

All this is fine for man 'called to create liberating structures', for 'homo oeconomicus', for working man, altering the environment, purposefully active towards a social end. For the unemployed, there is no 'haleness, being whole', no 'saving health', no 'healing and making whole of each'. There is only loss, emptiness, non-fulfilment, sickness of mind. We shall study instances of the tragedy of unemployment in succeeding chapters. As he thinks of such deprived persons as the unemployed, Schillebeeckx implicitly rebukes us all, including the employed who may consider themselves 'saved': 'There can be no talk of individualistic salvation. . . . Salvation is wholeness, and no man is made whole so long as disaster and oppression, injustice and misery prevail around him'.[40] Disaster, injustice and the misery of unemployment do so presently prevail around us. For all this, we are all, especially those of us who are employed, under the judgement of God.

I believe the contribution of Edward Schillebeeckx to modern theology to be of great importance, and I believe him to be all too little read. I believe that, while accepting that theology from above which gives some authority to texts and encyclicals, he allows that insights into God and his will for man also emerge from within man's God-orientated mind to bring him nearer to truth. I have seen the eyes and sensed the minds of students and of professors of theology in Oxford as they were directed towards what Schillebeeckx had to tell us there of his personal insights into God and God's saving will for man. There are amongst Christians some of us who believe that his teaching has given us a new understanding of the importance of earthly things in the process of human salvation. Man's eternal salvation may well begin with his opportunities for creativity, for responsibility, for understanding, for relationships on the shop floor. Deprive him in unemployment of these opportunities, leave him to wither, to rot, unwanted and useless in deprivation of work, and God knows the harm done to that person. The Bible knew nothing of the problem of unemployment, and texts cannot help us 'from above'. However, the implications of its teaching worked out 'from below' by thoughtful men are terrible and challenging indeed. Hard theologizing by many seems to be needed to stir towards endeavour apathetic but nominally Christian people who continue to tolerate unemployment and who are beginning to accept it as a permanent element in a technologically-orientated society. Bishop David Jenkins wrote:

> The motivation of radical politics is not to fit men and structures into a pattern already ideologically understood but to break out of structures ideologically determined and to set free human beings who are structurally and ideologically confined. The aim is that more people should get more space to be human and in this shall be able to perceive and create signs and foretastes of that full development of human reality which lies, as we Christians would put it, in the kingdom.[41]

The Bishop is connecting his theologizing 'from below' with the conception of the kingdom of God given us 'from above' in the Bible. There must indeed be a 'breaking out of structures ideologically determined' if those 'structurally and ideologically confined' are to be set free. I say in the name of God, basing myself upon theology 'from above' and 'from below', that every Christian ought to concern himself with the elimination of mass unemployment.

NOTES

1 Unless otherwise stated, all biblical quotations are from the *New English Bible*.
2 Catholic Truth Society, p. 87.
3 *The Biblical Doctrine of Work*, SCM Press, 1963, p. 25 (1st published 1962).
4 *On Genesis*, Geoffrey Chapman, 1977, p. 24.
5 *Old Testament Theology*, Volume 1, Oliver & Boyd, 1962, p. 145. (Original 1st German publication, 1956).
6 *The Social Psychology of Work* (op. cit.), p. 186.
7 *Laborem Exercens* (op. cit.), p. 85.
8 ibid., p. 87.
9 ibid., pp. 91-2.
10 ibid., p. 92.
11 ibid., p. 11.
12 *The Workers Charter*, Catholic Truth Society, 1958.
13 *Laborem Exercens* (op. cit.), p. 8.
14 ibid., p. 64.
15 C. H. & W. M. Whiteley: *The Permissive Morality*, Methuen, 1964, p. 43.
16 A. Louth: *Theology and Spirituality*, SLG Press, 1978, p. 5.
17 *Christ*, SCM Press 1980, p. 45 (1st published in Dutch 1977).
18 ibid., p. 50.
19 *New Fire*, Spring 1982, p. 12.
20 *Jesus*, Collins, 1979, p. 632 (1st published in Dutch 1974).
21 *Christ* (op. cit.), pp. 55/6.
22 Quoted from *World Faiths Insight*, London, Summer 1982.
23 *Annual Report for 1981*, pp. 10-11.
24 *New Fire*, Spring 1982, p. 12.
25 *The Observer*, 14 March 1982, p. 8.
26 *New Light on Social Problems*, Catholic Truth Society, 1961, p. 41.
27 From 'As Kingfishers catch fire'.
28 *Systematic Theology*, Vol. 1, Nisbet 1953.
29 *The First Assembly of the WCC*, SCM Press, 1949, p. 75.
30 *Vatican Council II*, Pillar Books, USA, 'Church in the Modern World', paras. 35 & 67.
31 *Ministry*, SCM Press, 1981, p. 5 (1st published in Dutch, 1980).
32 *Christ*, op. cit., p. 46.
33 ibid., p. 47.
34 ibid., p. 55.
35 *Christ* (op. cit.), p. 45.

36 *Jesus* (op. cit.), p. 627.
37 ibid., p. 633.
38 *Jesus* (op. cit.), pp. 24, 184, 656, 513.
39 *Christ* (op. cit.), p. 903.
40 ibid., p. 881.
41 *The Contradiction of Christianity*, SCM Press, 1976, p. 113.

6

The Unemployed

At the time of writing (in 1985) the total of registered unemployed in Great Britain is 3,272,565. The seasonally adjusted figure for the number of adults unemployed, excluding school-leavers, is 3,177,200. It is commonly held that, in addition to the registered unemployed, there are at least another 100,000 unregistered persons out of work. More than 6,000,000 people are at present dependent upon social security benefits. In Northern Ireland, more than 123,000 persons are out of work, that is to say 21.3% of the total workforce. In the Northern Region of Britain, over 226,000 are unemployed, that is to say 17.8% of the workers. Early in 1985, the unemployed of Great Britain as a whole comprised 13% of the workforce. The unemployment in Maryport in Cumbria is 30% in 1985. Of the present unemployed, the most recent figure available is that of 1,276,000 for those who have been out of work for more than a year, that is to say 39.6% of the total number of unemployed. These are figures which ought to be considered very seriously. They suggest a tragic national situation, an alarming prospect. The fact that so many researchers (and politicians) seem resigned to the likelihood of the figures remaining high for some years to come must not lead us to share in a tolerance for an altogether intolerable situation. Let me repeat as strongly as I am able that the miners went on strike in 1984, not because they hated work or hated the bosses, but because they feared with all their hearts that if they did not do something about it they would lose their jobs.

I have tried already to show why mass unemployment is humanly tragic. I have drawn attention to the psychological, social, philosophical, theological importance of work for the individual, of his need for that purposive activity with social significance which a paid job and other kinds of work (including some non-stipendiary work) provides for him. I have tried to show how work helps to develop and fulfil him, indeed to save him. My purpose has been to show how much he is missing, how liable indeed he is to dehumanization, if he is unemployed (or in any other way deprived of work). I propose now to try to look hard at unemployment, in the hope that I myself and others may be more effectively challenged to try to do something constructive about it. I am aware, however, of a criticism which may be made concerning what I have written up to this point. The criticism is that some work, especially some paid employment, is not in fact fulfilling, is not humanizing. It, too, like unemployment, is destructive, dehumanizing. I do not believe this to be true of the greater part of human work. However, in so far as there is any truth in the allegation, I propose in chapter 9 to discuss unhappiness at work and to suggest remedies.

There is amongst many in all classes of society considerable ignorance (and some prejudice) concerning the unemployed. I am told today of the young man who recently applied for a job, but who made it quite plain at his interview with his prospective employer that he did not really want the job. This kind of story gets around. Some time ago a lady in the Cotswolds wrote to the local paper to ask why 'all these layabouts living on social security' did not start to try to find some honest work. She was typical of those who do not understand the extent of unemployment and who judge the unemployed by the relatively few depraved persons amongst them. It is not true that there is work for the asking for it. She should have been present in the West Midlands town (not so far from the Cotswolds) when the BBC reporter saw five hundred people turn up for fifteen temporary jobs which had not even been publicly advertised. In the autumn of 1984, there were in Britain 5,500 job vacancies for 'general labourers'. There were 863,200 'general labourers' on the unemployment register.

The Cotswolds lady was answered with a wise gentleness in the columns of the same journal. She had the grace to apologize and withdraw. Yet one hardly knows how, in the face of such genuine ignorance, to write calmly and convincingly of unemployment, without sentimentality and repetitiveness. Let me begin by quoting two unprejudiced persons. I was in the pleasant home recently of a young E.E.T.P.U. senior shop steward and convener. The children were obviously well cared for and were surrounded by all that a child's heart could desire. The wife admitted that she was not politically minded, that her heart was not really in her husband's union activities. Suddenly in the midst of quiet talk, she burst out, 'This is an unfair society'. She had become overwhelmed for a moment with the consciousness of the suffering of close relatives and friends who were unemployed. For her, there was no personal experience; but she had knowledge of what those close to her were enduring.

Secondly, let me quote Bill Daniel, Senior Research Fellow of the Policy Studies Institute, and Adviser to the House of Lords Select Committee on Unemployment. This is what he said to us at a non-political conference (on counselling) in Liverpool:

> Unemployment is not a condition that falls uniformly across all sections of the community, nor even a condition that strikes in a random way across the working population as a whole. Unemployment falls disproportionately upon the low paid, the unskilled and those who are handicapped by poor health and disability. Unemployment can be seen as a tax levied upon the weakest, the poorest and the most deprived sections of the community.

This was not written for the popular press; nor was it part of a political speech. It was, however, a solemn indictment by a highly responsible and informed person of a society which sometimes seems ignorant of the sheer pain of unemployment, sometimes unaware of the utterly involuntary nature of most of it. Indeed Professor Chris Freeman, of Sussex University, declares emphatically that the rise in unemployment is no 'voluntary' phenomenon, represents no outbreak of 'scrounging'. Unemployment, he assures us, is 'overwhelmingly involuntary'.[1] The Department of Health and Social Security, reporting on supplementary benefits, stated that people are:

> now remaining unemployed for longer and having a lower earnings potential than in normal circumstances such as have obtained over the last 30 years. Despite this, we found very little evidence that they are declining to return to work and prefer to remain on benefit when jobs are offered to them.[2]

The Supplementary Benefits Commission itself has stated:

> The majority of the jobless are not unemployed of their own choosing. For most their condition is the result of outside events over which they have no control.

I have to labour at answering those allegations of unwillingness to work which are so frequently made and allegations of fraud on a vast scale among the unemployed.

It is easy to make these allegations; there is a minimum of truth in them; and to believe them quietens the consciences of people who ought to be most terribly concerned about the numbers of the unemployed and their state. Let us have a look at some of the Cotswold lady's 'lay-abouts on social security'. Here is 'Johnnie'. Perhaps the uninformed might call him 'a scrounger'. Certainly he is concerned to try to maintain for his family a decent standard of living. Johnnie is middle-aged; he was suddenly last year made redundant. His wife does part-time work. They have three rapidly growing children. He is humiliated by unemployment; he loses his self-respect. He is a good odd-job man, able to do anything from plumbing to painting. Lots of odd jobs come his way; he takes them. He is breaking the law because he is 'on the dole'; his conscience is uneasy; but at least some semblance of his living standard is maintained, his time is partially occupied; he can hold his head high (to a certain extent). He may be condemned as 'a moonlighter', but scarcely as a 'layabout'. He hungers and pines for 'honest work', for 'a real job'. The number of 'scroungers' and 'layabouts' is relatively few. Since early 1980 the Government has been taking steps to deal with 'wilful failure to take up job vacancies' and 'claiming benefit as an unemployed person while gainfully employed'. 1,050 extra staff were originally employed by the DHSS to deal with these menaces to social integrity. During 1980-1 the total Department of Health and Social Security personnel employed on this fraud-detecting work was 5,600.[3] During 1980, 7,900 persons were disqualified from unemployment benefit for refusing suitable employment.[4] The additional staff was taken on in 1980-1 to investigate not only failure to take up job vacancies but also failure to maintain dependent members of families who then had to claim supplementary benefit. As a result, £40 million was saved. The Manpower Services Commission issued in March 1982 a booklet on *Hidden Economies and Hidden Work*. It cautioned against the acceptance of various estimates concerning fraudulent claims by the unemployed. It referred to the Rayner study report which suggested a minimum level of 8% for fraudulent claims for supplementary allowance amongst the unemployed.[5] The EETPU Research Department reports:

Far from fiddling the system, many unemployed people do not claim everything they are entitled to. Although the number of unemployed eligible for supplementary benefit has increased, there has been a slight fall in the proportion of the eligible unemployed who claim. Anti-scrounging campaigns are likely to make this problem worse because many genuine claimants will be frightened to claim.[6]

Many people simply do not understand what they have a right to have. There is real difficulty for many in comprehending what is in print. A DHSS official, when asked by a friend of mine to make more plain what is available for the unemployed on social security, replied that 'we are not here to advertise'. Another, when faced last week with the dyslexic young Nicky's request for help in filling up a form, answered that 'we are not here to fill in your forms for you'. The scandal lies not so much in some receiving by fraud what the unemployed are not entitled to, but in the fact that many in great need and fully entitled to benefit do not apply for it and go without it.

In a 1980 report from Belfast it was found that 27% of children entitled to free school meals were not getting them; only 33% of those eligible for family income supplement were receiving it; and only 54% of those eligible for rent rebates, rate rebates and rent allowances were receiving them. All this lack of 'take up' is owing to difficulty in understanding non-verbal communications.[7] It is the very opposite of fraud. For the three (and more) millions of the unemployed who are honest, the struggle to pay electricity bills and to afford children's shoes remains. When 180 jobs as porters, cleaners, maids and kitchen workers were on offer in 1982, there was a queue of 3,500 applicants for them in below zero temperatures outside a Glasgow hotel.[8] Surely the human heart ought to break, the will stiffen, to help to right the wrongs of the unemployed in their ignorance and in their misery.

Unemployment is a shock when it falls upon the worker. It is frightening and depressing as its full significance sinks in; it is demoralizing as it goes on. Years ago I remember with pain the whiteness of Albert's and Cyril's faces when they lost their jobs. I saw in them the draining of hope, the fear that this was the beginning of the end, that they might never work again. Those white faces struck me as a young man with horror and filled me with pity. Then there was young Billy, the pride of his family, with his fine Grammar School education. He hid himself away day after day, lest the neighbours came to realize that he had no job. The Centre for Urban and Regional Development Studies at Newcastle upon Tyne University reported in August 1982 on BBC North—East Television that some school-leavers are never likely to get a job, and that many older persons who have lost their jobs will never find another. Michael Williams is a Welsh industrial chaplain. He tells how the unemployed sink into apathy. They give up fixing the fence and doing the mother-in-law's garden. They could have helped to build the community hall he was trying to get built. But they had passed the stage when they would have jumped at that.[9] They had lost heart. The long-term unemployed just tend to stay at home or hang around. An unemployed woman, bereft after fifteen years of regular work, says that in unemployment she does not know what to do with herself all day long. The young man who comes from an upper working class family and who has written 58 job applications without even gaining an interview will not now go out of the house because he is so ashamed of himself.[10]

'Henry' is fifty-seven. He has been at work all his life until two years ago. I have known him for much of that life. At fifty-five, he was shocked at the Employment Office and what he found there. No one tried to humiliate him; but he was inevitably humiliated. He seemed to have little chance of a job. He bought cheap strong tobacco, made up his own cigarettes; he smokes too much. Finally he broke into his electricity meter and made a couple of attempts at suicide. Now he has a job, a rather insecure and badly paid one. But he is alive again, a man again. Mrs A. is unemployed (at 54). Her husband is on a pension. She has four sons at home. They have sausages for Sunday dinner. Bacon and fish and meat, she says, are things of the past. They have onion sauce with their sausages.[10] They are not starving. However, as *The Guardian* says, 'they will have to choose between the gas bill and new shoes for the children, or new shoes and a hot meal and the electricity bill.'[11] Unemployment wears one down as it goes on. A personal friend tells me that when it came to him he just sat down and wept for half an hour. Even at the beginning of it, he had some idea of what it would come to mean for him and his family in the end.

Let me write something of my friend Nick. This is a Liverpool

Nick (not an Oxford one). He does not mind his name being used. He has some CSEs, some O-levels and an A-level in music. He is aged twenty-seven. He has been out of work for four years. He is active in the local Campaign for Nuclear Disarmament. Otherwise he has nothing to do. He gets up late and goes to bed late (after listening to the record player). He does not feel well; sometimes he feels physically ill. He will not go to the doctor because he will only give him anti-depressants. He is thin, eats sparingly, is a vegetarian. He feels that transport should be heavily subsidized, so that persons of limited income could afford occasional changes of scenery. He finds that the D.H.S.S. gives him a sense of inferiority. The offices, he says, are under-staffed. He believes that the whole system needs simplification. He is highly rational, sensitive, fantastically honest. He does not find it easy to talk about himself. However, these are some of the things he managed to say over a three week period. I have tried to knit them adequately together:

The position of the unemployed person is analogous to that of a victim of physical violence. Such a victim is too preoccupied with personal distress to be of value to those administering aid. . . . It seems to be of the nature of unemployment that it isolates its victims. They have no influential access to powerful organizations who have the bargaining power to improve their lot. Lack of frequent contact with people seems most likely to focus one's attention on one's own predicament. There is a gradual gravitation towards self-preoccupation. A rift or demarcation between the advantaged and the disadvantaged has been established. At first I regarded being unemployed as something of an enforced holiday. I did not consider it to be a 'dangerous occupation'. Then I began to question myself. Was I entirely at fault? I began to experience dilemmas of self-accusation. Much later, when the degree of skill which I had acquired was diminishing through lack of opportunity to exercise it, the question of why I was unemployed became less important. It seemed likely that the longer I remained unemployed the less employable I would become. By this time I had ceased to regard myself as having a skill, since circumstances had dictated its decline. In due course, the capacity in which I was registered at the Job Centre was altered to 'general worker'. The situation was evidently one in which the fittest would survive at the expense of the weakest, and I had misgivings about confronting it. Not only have I never been offered any general work; I have had no offer of any work whatsoever. At times I came to regard myself as one of the weakest that was actually going to the wall, and it seemed an uncivilized system to be part of. . . . There comes a time in the life of a young person in 20th century Britain when to live in too close proximity with his parents must damage and bastardize the relationship. The parents are unable to live as they wish, and the children have their healthy impetuosity disarmed and the development of their personalities loosely orientated around a generation they do not belong to. Even were it possible to secure a loan to establish my 'independence', debt to an unemployed person is like a slip-knot around the neck. There are no realistic conditions under which I would consider going into debt. There is a certain amount of pride in this; but there is also common sense based on past experience. I once expressed myself along these lines to a DHSS official. I was told that the DHSS was 'not in the business of setting single people up in flats'. It is cheaper to support people in families than living separately. These complex deliberations are not always so concrete in my awareness, but they subtly condition almost every other reflex. They submerge into a sea of inactivity which results from a burgeoning sense of futility and impotence. There is no perceivable 'centre' to my existence, no focal point around which everything revolves. There seems to be no action and consequential reaction, no development, no foundation, no trend, no peak. No energy is created and therefore none is dissipated. There is no forced exercise of a pattern, no rhythm, no accent. There is no responsibility.

From time to time I force projects upon my dying wits. But such attempts ultimately bore me, because they should be the natural counter-balancers of systematically organized or imposed activity such as one would find in a job. There one might work in a team, to meet deadlines, in real situations. These projects or hobbies lose meaning outside a situation based on more regimented activity. The enthusiasm for them wanes.

In certain increasingly rare situations when I find myself required to be sociable, I suddenly see that facets of my personality are moribund. One finds it difficult to speak, not only out of self-consciousness but out of difficulty in articulating words. The sounds of one's own voice seem strange. The sudden realization that you might no longer be able to make people laugh can cause involuntary reactions. You become humourless and unlaughing yourself. The formation and development of relationships become remote possibilities or nostalgic preoccupations. One's thoughts recede deeper inside oneself. Company becomes overpowering. One gradually comes to prefer solitude, and one becomes introverted and unrealistic. I have never developed a standard of living which extends much beyond bare essentials: tobacco, occasional transport expense to visit friends, a cheap paperback once every two or three weeks, or going to a football match. There is little left for anything else. The clothes I wear, though not shabby, are all remnants of my days as a student. To save money is difficult; when I have needed to do so it has taken as much as three months to accumulate £20. My parents buy shoes for me. Much of the work now available on the jobs market is of a self-employed contract type, which offers no security, no minimum wage, and requires an initial investment. Any other type of work offered (and there is not much) always asks for experience. At times I have resorted to extreme persuasion and half-myths to gain work. I have offered 'interest in the work', 'willingness to work hard' and to 'learn quickly'. Employers are suspicious of people expressing over-eagerness. To travel to London to apply for a job would involve debt. The vicious circle of debt which the unemployed dread more than any other has been entered. I am in a precarious position. One of the greatest fears I have as an unemployed person is of exacerbating the situation.

Unemployed people have principles. I have no general animosity for employed people; but there is certainly frustration at the lack of understanding on the part of people who have never been unemployed. I find myself becoming increasingly critical of the faceless system which makes and takes away work. How can I understand what unemployment does to me? I cannot cope. Most of the time one is occupied with oneself. I suffer nausea, claustrophobia, demon panic. I have only myself to contemplate. I can't cope with the vast empty spaces in my life.

Now he has at last left home, found a friend to live with. She works, he scrapes by. He is no neurotic, but simply an unemployed young person, after years of unemployment.

Mary is unemployed too, an unemployed trained social worker. She agrees with Nick, although she is relatively new to unemployment. Her husband is unemployed too. She understands the shoe problem. Your shoes must be decent if you apply for a job, if you go out anywhere. People judge you by your shoes. But how do you get them, when they cost so much? Ought you to get them when so much else is needed? She is humiliated (or rather angered) by the fact that she, a trained woman, a responsible would-be working woman, cannot get dental treatment unless her husband signs the form for her; she cannot obtain free school meals for her children without her husband's signature. Theirs is a united and devoted family; yet she finds herself beginning to feel insignificant. Her husband sometimes get a little supply teaching. Then she is alone, the two children at school. Why bother to clean the house, why bother to dress for another empty day? Why bother to cook, to eat, when so little energy is needed? She gets over these feelings; but they come all the same. Unemployment tends to lead into introspection of an unhealthy kind. Often she says, the life of the unemployed becomes meaningless. She herself is a fine wife and devoted mother. She has a real sense of vocation to others besides her own family. It is, of course, unfulfilled.

There is for the unemployed, at least for the long-term unemployed, real danger of their losing their own self-respect. When that happens, of course anything can happen. A Roman Catholic priest, a writer on ethics, says that 'there comes a time when living is no longer human life'.[12] That is what I have been trying to say. J. Moltmann defined freedom as 'initiation, creativity, a passion for the future'. For the unemployed there is little scope for initiation and creativity, fear rather than passion for the future. Moltmann tells us that 'to be used and needed . . . gives life meaning'. The life of the unemployed is meaningless, for he is un-used and seemingly under present circumstances un-needed. He tends to withdraw into what Moltmann calls 'closed-in-ness'; indeed he is forced into it. Moltmann writes: 'I am free and feel myself to be free when I am respected and recognized by others . . . I become truly free when I open my life for other people and share with them, and when other people open their lives for me and share them with me.'[13] There is nothing really to be shared in unemployment; one is afraid of offering the unemployed person a drink, lest he feel obliged to offer one back, to share what he cannot afford. He may be respected, but he finds that difficult to believe. Kant said that friendship combines affection with respect. The unemployed person seems to himself to be losing respect and friends.

Dennis is a thinker. He puts what he thinks onto a borrowed type-writer for me. He has had a lot of time lately in which to think about what has been happening to him, what has been happening within him. Now, temporarily, just for another month, he has a job. He writes (and I shall drastically cut down what he has written, because Nick has said such a lot):

Dad had sometime mentioned the dole queues of the 1930s which, with the myths and folk-tales of endless newspaper supplements, did not prepare me for the first step of unemployment – signing-on. If any tyrant wished to devise a simple system of knocking the stuffing out of people and making them toe-the-line, he should visit an Unemployment Benefit Office. . . . Everything is done in a queue, with only an occasional sop to privacy; there is a wafer-thin board between lines. My signing-on office was huge and bare; voices echoed everywhere, and no matter when I went there were always a few hundred people just waiting around. That first visit took most of the day and all I had to do was to answer half-a-dozen questions and sign a form. From then on it was every alternate Monday at 9.40am.

With earnings related benefit I received enough for rent and food. Exceptional needs payments were no longer available; so I had to start buying my clothes at jumble sales. Most of my food was bought from a market stall that dealt with the stuff that no one else wanted – broken fish-fingers and squashed 'meat' pies. It was cheap.

Dennis learned in a way to cope. He made work for himself, did some voluntary church work, took his Open University course. That was good; but Open University work does not last for ever and it lacks social significance. As I have tried to show earlier, work does not satisfy unless it has social significance. Man does not, cannot, live for himself alone. I have tried to write what is real, about the inmost feelings of real (and honest) people. Before I write about some of the practical problems arising from unemployment, let me say something concerning a sort of 'success story'.

Martin Rathfelder was, when I saw him last, a happy unemployed person. He illustrates my theme that by work I do not mean only paid employment. Martin was unemployed, and he was not paid; but he was a worker. He had been unemployed for quite a time. He is still in his early twenties. He told me: 'I don't feel like an unemployed person. I'm enjoying myself.' He was single and lived at home. This helped him to live relatively comfortably. His secret of 'unemployment without tears' was that he did regular work during regular working hours each day of the week. For four days he worked behind the counter of the local Citizens' Advice Bureau. He enjoyed the work and found it rewarding. He is purposefully active towards social ends. On the fifth day he worked the same hours cleaning and decorating in the newly-acquired Unemployment Centre. He was (as anyone could see as Martin went off to work in his jeans) a working man. He was accepted as such. He was no 'drop out' or 'throw out'; he was a needed man, a useful man; he held his head high. If he spent the same time each day decorating his home, it would not be 'real work'. He would indeed be altering the environment, satisfying the urge for activity (and creative activity at that). However, the work (at home) would not be sufficiently social; it would be too domestic. A worker 'goes' to work. He would be staying at home. He would lose respect for himself, however useful the decorating. He is a social being. So Martin, the unemployed man, worked and was satisfied, although he received no pay. What he did, unlike what the 'moonlighter' does, was honest and above board. He respected himself cheerfully, and he was immensely respected. I have lost touch with him. One wonders about his future; he might want to marry. His funds were low.

Let us look again at Henry. He was fifty-five during his last (and only) period of unemployment. He said that it was terrible not to have to go out in the morning. He says that if you are unemployed you must stick to a routine, rise regularly and early as if you are wanted for something. Otherwise, he says, you just lie in, and you crack. All this is made worse by the common undernourishment of the unemployed. Many single men like Henry tend to be bad domestic managers. They do not live on a balanced diet with an eye to the calories. Sometimes their fortnight's benefit and social security payment are gone before the fortnight ends. I succeeded at one time in having our Leslie paid weekly. He has no idea of how to divide either in his mind or on paper what he receives. Consequently his money runs out before the fortnight ends. It is, alas, not much better when he is kindly paid weekly. He just does not get enough (for him). The problem of obtaining necessary new clothes is a major one for him. In particular he needs new boots. Applying for grants is a difficult proposition for him. It takes not only time and effort, but that slight intellectual capacity which he does not possess. He gets sandwiches at two convent doors to 'see him through' the fortnight (or the week). The Bishop of Stepney and the (Roman Catholic) Bishop in N. London report that social security offices cannot cope with the vast increases in their work. Consequently, they tell us, many unemployed have to wait for six days to receive the money to which they are entitled. Because sufficient hostel accommodation is not available, many young have nowhere to sleep but the streets.[14]

'Jack' uses the streets in summer. In winter he uses the 'shelters', or the public lavatories (where these are kept open and warmed). He carries his spare shoes and clean socks neatly packed with his razor and sleeping-bag in a light hold-all wherever he goes. Also he carries a clock. In the shelters are food and a bed; but there are no bathing facilities. He can wash face and hands in the public toilets, but it is a problem to find where he can wash his feet. He cannot get a job till he gets a 'fixed abode'. He cannot get a room till he gets the money for the deposit. When, sometimes, with social security help, he does get a room, he does not feel that, in unemployment, he can stay in it all day. Then, inevitably, he is tempted to spend money, like the other people who are out. He likes, if he can, to have one square meal a day. He has no vices. However, he does like to go in for 'spotting the ball'. He has twice won £10 as third prize for his skill. He does, too, like to put a little money on the horses. He very much enjoys a beer last thing at night, when he can afford it. Of course, social security was not designed for this. He does not complain, but wonders what he could do with his time that would not cost money. Occasionally, he gets depressed, but on the whole is getting used to this sort of life. He has no family or home. He is thirty-three, rational, intelligent and fit. He sometimes gets washing-up jobs.

People say that there will never be work for all. Let us look, therefore, at the case for 'the alternative society', where it is assumed that many (millions) will never have jobs. They will have to be adequately supported by the state, and they must be educated and trained for cultural and other leisure activities. This kind of suggestion was made as long ago as the 1930s by the Rev. P. E. T. Widdrington (of the Christendom Group of Christian social thinkers). It is no practicable solution. The alternative society will not work, because it will not provide work. The amateur painter does not gain the satisfaction and fulfilment of the professional. The idle rich, so far as their memoirs reveal them, do not seem to have been conspicuously happy. I had for six years the task of assisting a considerable number of boys from an élitist school to decide what to do immediately after leaving that school. They had all had an excellent education, with personal tuition and small classes. They had also had exceptional opportunities for learning the arts: painting, pottery, sculpture. They were well trained for cultural and other leisure activities. The great object of their young lives, despite their parents' more than adequate means (in most cases), was to get work. I was amazed time and again that they were so little concerned about what they would be paid for that work.

Those who advocate the alternative society, the society of cultural and leisured pursuits in place of work, are not the unemployed but people who are themselves at work. Mostly they sit at desks and can imagine a leisured future in which they have that time to read which they at present lack. The unemployed are not like that. John Wellens refers to a survey of a group of young people with extra opportunity for leisure on their hands. They were asked how they had spent this time, how they had used this opportunity during a considerable period. The answers came through loudly and clearly: resting, relaxing, loafing. In fact, as Mr Wellens concludes, they had done nothing.[15] A young driver from Didcot told me recently of his days of enforced unemployment. 'It was terrible just to sit and look out of the window.' He has work now. Culture and leisure activities are fine if you have work. 'Abdul' has a great deal of secondary and tertiary education. He is a civil engineer. He is not without culture, comes from a cultured environment. He sits around the house. He will not decorate or dig, will not read. He sits and envies his wife who goes out to work. He wants a job and would go anywhere for one. Tonight, as I write, a woman of forty-one rings up to ask if I can tell her how to get work at an old people's home. 'I would cook or anything,' she says. She says she would work 'for £2.00 or anything'. She has plenty of culture and some money. She makes it plain that what she really wants is work. That is how people are.

A letter from Dennis lies in front of me. His fifty-three weeks of unemployment are over, he writes. He says: 'I am back to my normal self . . . I found myself singing in the bath last night . . . something I haven't done for over a year!' Unemployment has not meant starvation for him; it has meant degradation. The Supplementary Benefits Commission reported to Parliament as long ago as 1978:

To keep out of poverty people must have an income which enables them to participate in the life of the community. They must be able, for example, to keep themselves reasonably fed, and well enough dressed to maintain their self-respect and to attend interviews for jobs with confidence. Their homes must be reasonably warm; their children should not feel shamed by the quality of their clothing; the family must be able to visit relatives and give them something on their birthdays and at Christmas time; they must be able to read newspapers, and retain their television sets and their membership of trade unions and churches. And they must be able to live in a way which ensures, so far as possible, that public officials, doctors, teachers, landlords and others treat them with the courtesy due to every member of the community.

The Senior Registrar in Community Medicine in the Department of Epidemiology and Social Research in the University Hospital of South Manchester writes:

It seems extremely likely that unemployment is a health-damaging status. . . . We know that life-changes damage health until the individual readjusts, and we know that losing your job is a life-change and that you are not supposed to adjust to worklessness. We know that social networks are important to health and that the unemployed lose the social network of work and also that they withdraw from other social obligations because of stigma and lack of money. . . . The weight of evidence points strongly towards an adverse health effect of unemployment.[16]

I must conclude with further reference to two perennial problems of the unemployed: shoes and electricity bills. When the Bishop of Durham mentioned the need of an unemployed family in 1985 for children's shoes, the comfortably off derided him. For unemployed couples, the problem of children's shoes seems never-ending. For Mick, who does not kick footballs, a new pair of shoes is necessary every six or eight months. He walks everywhere, has to walk everywhere. As long ago as 1978, nearly £10 million was owed to the Electricity Service in Northern Ireland. Sometimes as many as a thousand homes a month are having their electricity disconnected in Southern Scotland for non-payment of accounts. It is recognized that the three main causes of poverty are retirement, single parenthood and unemployment.

I listened on Television News to the account of a survey.

Twenty-seven per cent of those canvassed thought things 'fairly good'. They need waking up. All who have begun to realize what life is like for the unemployed ought to engage in reasoned dialogue, encourage detailed research, strive with reason and will to put an end to it. The Rhonnda Valley boy who had six months of unemployment when he was seventeen had had more than enough of it. Then for two years he trained and worked at Rhonnda Enterprises of Porth. He swept the floor, perfected his tap wrench, rode home on his motor-bike like a king.

NOTES

1   *The Microelectronics Revolution*, ed. T. Forester, Basil Blackwell, 1980, p. 311.
2   EEPTU Research Department *Shop Stewards Quarterly Review*, April 1980, p. 12.
3   House of Commons (Hansard) *Parliamentary Debates*, Vol. 4, No. 97, 8 May 1981, Column 79.
4   *The Guardian*, 23 Nov. 1982, p. 1.
5   Para. 3, 17.
6   *Shop Stewards Quarterly Review* (op.cit.), p. 13.
7   *Poverty*, April 1980, p. 6.
8   *The Guardian*, 9 January 1982, p. 4.
9   *New Society*, 2 September 1982, p. 381.
10   *The Guardian*, 8 January 1981, p. 8.
11   20 October 1981, p. 14.
12   R. A. McCormick: *How Brave a New World?*, SCM Press, 1981, p. 22.
13   *The Trinity and the Kingdom of God*, SCM Press, 1981, pp. 218, 219, 213, 216 (1st Published in Germany 1980).
14   *Church Times*, 3 December 1982, p. 1.
15   *Industrial and Commercial Training*, November 1981, p. 342.
16   *New Society*, 1 July 1982, p. 30.

7

The Unemployment of the Young

The current Youth Training Scheme is an attempt both to 'employ' and to train school-leavers, so that no sixteen year old boy or girl shall, if he or she cooperates, go from school straight into unemployment. Before its introduction, 'Patrick' had been six months out of school and out of work. While the other members of his family went to work each morning, he 'lay in'. He would get up about noon and play records until the rest of the family came home. Then he would go out for a while. He greatly wanted a job. He hoped that he might get a Y.O.P. job, looking after pensioners' allotments. He thought he had a good chance. He was a gentle boy. When he went out of his home and leaned against a wall, the police came along and told him to move on. He went and leaned against another wall, and they came again and told him again to move on. It was not much of a life for a sixteen year old. He was (and, I hope, still is) a law-abiding lad. He lives in Liverpool. From April 1986, there is to be two years of training on the Y.T.S.

When unemployed youth riot in Brixton or Bristol, it is partially at least because they have nothing else to do. They have 'an urge to alter the environment' (as the psychologist said). They get no chance to do this except by vandalism and rioting. I was dismayed by the spectacle of Railton Road, Brixton, on a peaceful shopping afternoon after the riots. People coming to and from the Brixton Covered Market passed hundreds of unemployed youths outside the decaying (or decayed) homes. They had nothing to do and were waiting for something to happen. They cannot watch television all day. In fact, many of them have lost interest in television. It is commonly understood that there are fifty youngsters chasing every job in some of the South London boroughs. Now, in 1985, new housing has gone up in Railton Road.

An Oxfordshire child panicked recently when sickness prevented her from going to school. It took time for her parents and teachers to discover that what was really on her mind was the fear that, if she did not attend school regularly, she would not get a job when she left school. She was eight years old. An Oxford Probation Officer is told by unemployed boys on probation that she cannot fool them. They will not get real jobs; they know it; she knows it.

After rioting in Manchester, police patrols and vans frequently toured the city at night, stopped youths, man-handled them, sometimes abused them, sometimes pushed them into a police vehicle to question them. They would be mostly those unemployed youngsters who did nothing all day and were full of energy at night. They were the unemployed, full of life and sick at heart, ready for anything. 'Unemployment on Moss Side', said the report, 'has had a devastating effect'. It suggested that continued youth unemployment was leading to eventual refusal to work and to criminal propensity.[1] It has indeed surprising effects. They are not surprising to the student of the sorely tried human mind. There is 'Paul', for example. He is eighteen, mature, greatly respected among his peers and his elders. He has an A-level and eight O-levels. He left school four months ago. He would have worked harder at school, if he had known that he would have been unacceptable at a university because he lacked the right A-levels (and unacceptable for a job because he lacked experience). He does not really blame anyone; but no-one seems to have prepared him for what would happen when he left school. Now his friends are back at school or out at work or seem to be hiding themselves. He is quite a tall fellow, but he feels small. Also he feels lonely and tired. Even the walk back from 'signing on' seems to tire him. He is tired of receiving letters which begin: 'I regret to inform you'. He is on waiting lists and goes on waiting. He dreads the question: 'What have you been doing with yourself all day?'. He finds 'the telly' boring. He does two nights a week on duty at the church bar. 'It makes me feel I'm doing something,' he says. He adds that work will feel like a holiday, if he ever gets it.

I am writing about juvenile unemployment in a separate chapter because of the extra-seriousness of the problem of the unemployment of the young. The moral degeneracy which often follows the humiliation and enforced inactivity of juvenile unemployment does harm to the individual which may be lasting. Ordinary parents do not know what to do to help. Professor Walter James, in pleading for 'new attitudes . . . to the provision of community services', writes: 'When our children ask for work, we give them the serpent of unemployment.'[2] Youngsters are often desperate to make themselves employable; some write scores of letters of application. At last, most terribly, many become resigned to it. A youngster of 18 says simply: 'I'm never going to get any work.' He knows it; he means it; it is certainly not what he wants. A small Welsh unemployed lad whom I met in the Rhonnda Valley told me that he was hoping for a job in the mines when he was nineteen. My heart sank for him. However, now he has his job. He is down the mine and on top of the world. He has come to life.

The bright eyes of the young of the Rhonnda Valley haunt me. Boys and girls are still mostly full of hope for work. Down at the Careers Office in Porth, Mrs Stewart told me that there are literally no jobs at all for the young. She insists that the young unemployed come in to see her each fortnight during their unemployment; but she has no jobs to offer. She says that the young do not seem to become depressed until after two years of unemployment. She says that 'merely living here in the Valley helps'. Apart from the Youth Training Scheme, some young people tend to stay on at school or go to the Technical College or the College of Further Education. That is not quite what they want; but it passes the time. Girls especially, Mrs Stewart says, seem to feel their lack of independence; they tend to resent, although mildly enough, their lack of earned money of their own. They do not have holidays away from the Valley (unless the church organizes some economical but fascinating camping holiday in France). They dread becoming lazy. They say so frankly again and again. It surprised me. They are all too aware of the unhappiness of the lazy. They do not want to marry young. However, it is not a great life to be without job or money or husband. Some of them lie in each morning during Technical College holidays; some deliberately do not lie in; they do not want to acquire bad habits. They try not to give way to depression; but they know that at the end of a year's secretarial training at the Technical College there is precious little prospect of a secretarial job. Mrs Stewart is wise and kind and understanding; but all that does not give her anything to offer.

In early 1985, according to Geoffrey Holland, Director of the Manpower Services Commission, of the 1.8 million young people aged 16 and 17, over one million had left full-time education. 350,000 were on the Youth Training Scheme, 420,000 were employed outside the Youth Training Scheme, 220,000 were unemployed and claiming social security, and 65,000 were 'inactive'.[3]

Some of the Welsh boys speak a little abrasively. 'Luke' says that now that he has not got a job he just cannot give so much time to voluntary work. He could, but he will not. That is how human nature works. The job has gone, and the heart has gone out of him with the job. There is no 'alternative (leisured) society' for him. 'Bill' had had two years at the College of Further Education. He was nineteen. He said that most of his school-mates were not working. 'Alan' was doing a diploma course in Business Studies at the Technical College. He felt that being there at twenty, when you ought to be out at work, 'makes you feel like a kid'. He personally would be happy enough to do a year of National Service. He said that he was 'just filling in time'. He did a few jobs about the house, helped to run the church youth club (especially the Disco). He said that to get a job would make a new man of him.

From September 1981, forty unemployed youngsters from the Coventry area were taken on by Jaguar Cars for nine months of intensive training. This followed detailed discussions between the Manpower Services Commission and British Leyland. The scheme was funded by the M.S.C. When it was first advertised in the Coventry Careers Office, more than fifty completed application forms were received by Jaguar Cars in two days. One hundred and fifty further applications followed. Those chosen were given work for six months in the Company's Radford engine plant, where they studied turning, milling, fitting, electronics, fabrication, technical drawing and stock communications skills such as report-writing and verbal presentations. For the last three months they moved on to the Browns Lane Jaguar Assembly Plant where they practised what they had learnt. During the whole nine months' training the youngsters attended day release classes of City and Guilds and Technical Education Council standard at local Colleges of Further Education and shared with the full-time Jaguar apprentices in community work.

Under the New Training Initiative, all sixteen year old school-leavers are offered a Youth Training Scheme place on a year's foundation training course. It aims to assess the capacities of youngsters, to try to ensure that they have such basic skills as literacy, and to give them both work experience and training at a company training centre or a College of Further Education. It reduces the number of boys and girls who go from school into unemployment. It does not cater for the unemployed in their late teens. The basic problem of youth unemployment remains. It is that of finding jobs which will both fulfil and last. The young want work which will give security and independence. The young person leaving school wants to achieve adulthood, to prove and satisfy himself. He does not want the transitory, the insecure.

With disappointment, the mind of the jobless young may turn suicidal. The case will be remembered by many of the two Widnes lads who killed themselves on 6 May 1981, when unemployment in Widnes was running at nearly 18 percent. They left a note for the *Widnes Weekly News:* 'What have we left in life now there's no work for anyone? All teenagers have to do is hang around street corners and walk up and down town, getting moved on by the police, who think you're getting up to something.' Doubt has been cast on their sincerity. Some of the Liverpool lads branded the suicide as 'daft'. Some Widnes boys claim that suicide is effeminate, and (like grief) 'weak'.[4] Dr Leslie Stephen, of Culham College Institute, took part in four years of research into the problems of London-based young people who came from 'every county save one', he told me. He found that of those aged between 16 and 25 who had been unemployed, 25 percent admitted that they had contemplated suicide during periods of unemployment.

In such a situation, much good counselling is vitally necessary. In large cities (and in some smaller towns) are persons and institutions which attempt to minister to the needs of young persons deprived of their right to work. Near the centre of one of Britain's largest cities, a Young People's Advisory Service (YPAS) is managed by a committee of local people concerned for the welfare of youth. By day it deals chiefly with unemployed teenagers (although some of its clients may just be taking a day off school). It has its counselling service which functions centrally, and an 'out-reach project' which involves small teams of youth counsellors who meet young people on their own ground: in public houses, in clubs, in record shops, in their homes. The centre itself is 'a drop-in centre'. There, when I last heard of it, was Steve, available every morning. Young people who dropped in could see him there, could query him, 'cheek' him, make outrageous statements, and then perhaps (out of the blue as it were) say 'I think I may be pregnant' (or anything else that might be on their minds). Steve was young and looked young. He looked tired. He knew of no solutions to young people's problems, had no magic remedies, had little self-confidence. But he was there, and he inspired confidence. People approached him who would not approach clergy or social workers. He just sat there in his jeans. He saw, he listened, he knew a thing or two, he was non-judgemental. He was, therefore, well placed to help. He was both young and strangely mature. He had known the unemployment of the young himself. He could help, knew what to say, when to say it. In the afternoon, there were groups. In the evening, he 'reached out' to the young contacts. There are others like him. But there are not enough.

By trying to make Steve real to the reader, I am trying to make the need real: the desperate need of the young unemployed. 'Work is healing to me,' a 22 year old unemployed girl said to me this morning. 'My life', she said, 'is in my work.' She asked if I could see what she meant. I could see all right. I am trying to explain how great is the need of the young without jobs to explode somehow, with all their pent up feelings of being unwanted, un-needed, un-used. Those who do not turn to rioting and vandalism are helped by people like Steve to pass the long days (and the longer nights).

Young unemployed persons have not the heart to do the house work or to decorate the home. Whatever heart they might have to help in their spare time when they are at work, for young people when they are not at work home becomes a place of shame, a place which should be empty during the working day. When they are in it, they have a feeling that they ought not to be there. They slip out of it when they have somewhere to go and the money needed to get there. The young unemployed care for the same recreational activities as the young employed. Many of them like to go to pubs. Bus (and train) fares are high. They cannot go far. The local pub provides a change of scene and company. There is a problem beyond that of getting there. It is that of standing a small round of drinks. Of course, friends are very considerate towards the unemployed. They do not expect them to stand rounds; but the embarrassment remains. They like to play pool or snooker. They want to use the space invader machines, the juke box. Some of them would like to go to football matches. These cost money. They buy records if they can. They make their own (thin) cigarettes. Apart from the pub, there is the neighbour's wall to lean against, provided that the neighbour does not chase one away.

All these domestic and social problems would solve themselves if they could get work. Without work, the young unemployed may become awkward customers. There is danger of their becoming anti-social. They are fish out of water; fish out of water lash out. Sue has given up hope after six weeks of being unable to find work. She says: 'There's no way I'm going to find a job. . . . I've really given up looking for a job now. . . . I envy people in work . . . girls in work seem to have so much more freedom; they can save up, get a flat, do anything.' She lacks work and lacks funds. She is frustrated, unfulfilled; the de-humanization process has begun.

Stuart is a big fellow; he plays football and cricket and does weight-lifting. There was a little trouble recently, and I went down to the Court for him and said that he was one of the best boys in Oxford. I meant it. His mother said to me, 'He's almost dead through feeling he's unwanted, as he's turned down for job after job'. Both unemployment and the fear of unemployment are disturbing. It is interesting that during the inner-city riots of 1981, two-thirds of the 4,000 arrested were under twenty years old. Only a minority of them were blacks.

Under unemployment, inevitably something happens to the young. It is in no sense for their good. Those who know them know the truth of what I am saying. Those who do not know them must try to understand. Only when the tragedy of the unemployment of the young is understood by a considerable number of persons will there begin to develop in the nation a sense that it cannot be tolerated, that it is truly unacceptable. Then and then only will responsible adults come to realize that the community will have to make sacrifices for the young. I shall say something of what this will mean in my last chapter. At present, I am asking only for hard and realistic thinking, not for sentimentality. On the whole poorly educated, jobless for considerable periods in their late teens, insecure, inevitably discontented: such are the young unemployed.

The (Conservative) Northern Ireland Secretary, in Parliament as long ago as 10 December 1982, referred to the young of the Province as 'frustrated by the prospect of unemployment for years ahead'. *The Scottish Bankers Magazine,* referring to an Organization for Economic Co-operation and Development Report, concludes that youth unemployment is likely to be a permanent phenomenon of the economy.[5] At a Jim Conway Foundation (trade union) seminar, an official from Durham stated that some of our children will never have jobs, will never know what work is. As his words sank down into us, we were all hurt. Surely as a community we ought not to tolerate such a state as this for our growing young adults. If ever there was a case for 'jobs for the boys' (in a literal, not a metaphorical sense), here it is now, whatever the cost may be to the rest of us.

NOTES

1 *The Guardian,* 13 July 1981, p. 2.
2 *The Times,* 4 June 1981, p. 15.
3 *Employment News,* January 1985, p. 1.
4 *The Observer* (Colour Supplement), 22 August 1982, p. 15.
5 February 1982, p. 137.

8

Towards Full Employment

Towards the end of 1984, approximately 12.75 million workers were unemployed in the countries of the European Economic Community, and the O.E.C.D. calculated that 20 million new jobs would be needed in the industrialized world to stop unemployment from rising even higher during the next few years.[1] In Britain, the unemployment rate in 1985 is 13.5 percent, almost double that of West Germany. This book is not written to say exactly how unemployment can be cured, the grievous wound in the social fabric healed. It is written only to say that the experts, and indeed the community as a whole, ought to be bending over backwards to see what can be done to cure it. This chapter, and the final chapter too, are attempts to show that the situation is not without hope, to say that some experts (and others) can see at least reasoned possibilities of a return towards full employment.

It is frequently said that the current development of micro-technology is bound to result in lasting unemployment. The micro-processor and the robot replace human labour. An I.T.V. programme tells us that 'the advent of the chip means that our children will grow up without jobs to go to'. All this is by no means certain. Trade union leaders have assured us that to fail to accept the challenge of the new technology is to sabotage our future as a nation. Lord Murray of Epping Forest, formerly of the TUC, tells us that the issue is simply how we can maximize the benefits of the new technology, minimize its costs and ensure that its benefits are equally shared.[2] Mr Terry Duffy, with all the professional care for workers that his leadership of the Amalgamated Union of Engineering Workers inevitably laid upon him, tells us that 'failure to accept the challenge of the new technology would . . . be to sabotage our national future'.[3] While advances in micro-electronics and the development of the computer chip are bound to make some human labour redundant, there may well be an absorption of that redundant labour in work generated by the industrial and commercial successes of the technological revolution. As the successful proprietor of a small industry dependent on much larger ones remarked to me last night, 'many fleas live on the big dog's back'.

It is vital for the future of Britain and its workers that this country should compete successfully with other countries and be in the forefront of that revolution. British manufacturing productivity still remains behind that of many of our competitors. This bodes ill for our industrial (and employment) future. Britain needs to increase its supply of production-based skills. It also needs the very maximum of automation. With increased automation and increased productivity, there will be increased competitiveness for British manufacturers. It should be possible to produce more goods more cheaply and to sell them on the markets of this country and the world. There will be the need for more skilled labour, and possibly (given success) for more labour altogether. For all this, the importance of training for the new technology becomes greater than seems as yet fully realized. The Manpower Services Commission commissioned a report in 1981 which stated (in 1982) that 'the introduction of new technology is essential for Britain under conditions of international competition'. It quoted one report which claimed that 'if output expands sufficiently fast, then labour can be reabsorbed in producing higher output'. In another report quoted by it, the effect of the development of micro-electronics might, with wage restraint and additional investment, create more jobs, many more jobs, than it dispenses with.[4] All realists on both sides of industry know, in fact, that the technological revolution has to go forward for the benefit of the whole community, including all those who work in it.

No country employs more technology than Japan. In addition to those firms there whose names have become known in every country to which the fruits of their mass production go, there are 7,000,000 small firms with average employment of only five or six persons. Toyota's 140 direct suppliers draw in turn upon no less than 40,000 sub-contractors. There is indeed no cause for despair concerning the impact of micro-technology. Professor Christopher Freeman, of the Science Policy Research Unit of the University of Sussex, writes that in the midst of depression 'growth starts again with a new wave of technical innovation'. He goes on to say that, with 'the diffusion of these basic innovations', perhaps even 'a decade or more' after them, there are 'powerful multiplier effects in generating additional demands on the economy for new capital goods, for components, for distribution facilities and of course for labour'.[5] Only 2·7% of the workers are unemployed in Japan (in 1985).

In our striving towards full employment, let us look now at that reflation without gross inflation which civilized men and women of many sections of the community are convinced is necessary for this country. This is the kind of work which will be financed nationally but which will lead towards a growth in national efficiency, productivity, economy. It is work which is needed for this country. For example, no-one who listens to the early morning radio can doubt that our road system is inadequate. There are 'repairs' and 'emergency repairs'; there is congestion; there is need for more motor-roads and for improvements to the ones we have. By-passes could be built, better access to ports provided, faster repairs carried out. Unskilled labour is required, and unskilled labour is available.

No-one is ignorant of the need for further investment in the railways. There ae 11,000 miles of railway network. There is a strong case for electrification of the main lines and for modernisation of the computer belt network. An improvement in rail-freight services would help to relieve congestion on the roads. An improved signalling system would have eliminated a recent accident on the railways, as British Rail has explained to us. 'A spokesman' says to us on television that 'we've never had the money to modernize our signalling equipment.' It is not only the shortage of money and labour available for repair and construction. It is in transport matters the seeming lack of forward planning for an efficient system which will help to promote an efficient economy. The South London Industrial Mission, situated close to Blackfriars Bridge, scarcely needs extensive research to give it cause to write that 'British Rail is slowly and steadily disintegrating through years of inadequate financing'. It pleads for the planning of transport nationally and locally. It declares (after considerable research):

To attain our aims some restriction of private privilege is essential in order to attain publicly efficient transport. In 1970 during the peak periods in London 12 percent of people commuted by car. These cars occupied 64 percent of the road space. If only half of that road space were released, a significant speed-up in bus services would occur. If fares were kept down and numbers of buses increased more people would leave cars behind. If cars were to be down-graded to their planned role and lose their privileged place, then still further progress could be made. Efficiency could be measured by our average speed in crossing Central London. This is approximately the same now as 100 years ago.

The cost of repairs to housing after flooding in such towns as York and Selby are so high as to make it seem absurd that we do not undertake the necessary land drainage and make these recurring costs unnecessary. The initial cost to the small town of Selby in the floods of 1982 was £50,000 for two days. This was only the beginning of the expense involved. It is true that the returns on capital expenditure for land drainage are difficult to measure. They are none the less real. It is not easy for the parties to make political capital out of such expenditure. Indeed public expenditure on construction works as a whole fell by thirty-five percent in volume between 1975-6 and 1981-2. Unemployment in the construction industry rose in the same period to a total of 370,000,[6] one quarter of the work force.

Council house building has been greatly reduced. The case for building houses and for repairing houses is evident to all who know our inner cities. Belfast, Toxteth (in the shadow of the great Cathedral), Railton Road haunt me. Who can tell whether this house or that house was damaged in the rioting or whether it has just decayed, disintegrated on its own? It pays no-one to repair it, to re-build it. It may be unoccupied or occupied; it is in either case only the ghost of a real house. In such houses all over Britain, some of them (because of unpaid bills) without heat or light, children are brought up. The Government's five-yearly English House Survey shows that, of 18.1 million homes in England, 1.1 million were unfit, 900,000 lacked basic amenities, a million required repairs costing more than £7,000 each. The Greater London Survey of 1981 showed that 10 percent of London's housing was unfit for human habitation and that 19 percent of it required repairs to the value of at least £3,000 per house.[7] It was grim to learn of polio in Belfast in 1982. On two estates it was claimed that the flats were rat-infested, that burst pipes had created pools of stagnant water, that sewers were blocked. Excrement had been seen seeping into gardens in the area. There were outbreaks of diarrhoea, and instances of hepatitis.[8]

According to the careful investigation of Giles Merritt, of *The Financial Times*, at least 300,000 new homes need to be built in Britain every year. Indeed, he claims that 380,000 would be a more sound target. This would be more than double the present level of building.[9] The present shortage of housing hinders the movement of labour to places where jobs (but not houses) are available. Giles Merritt writes: 'In Britain, housing experts believe that in order to allow true mobility of the workforce, the surplus of housing, known as the "vacancy reserve", would need to be of the order of ten percent, which in turn means that an extra 2 million homes would be required'.[10] It is a formidable figure; let it be at least a pointer towards need.

Under the roads of our cities are the sewers, less obvious. The sewerage system and its well-being is important to the health of all who live and work above it. It is well-known to many (but seemingly all too easily put out of mind for the present) how greatly the system is in need of repair, of modernization, indeed of reconstruction. Sir Terence Beckett, of the CBI, declared on 4 February 1983: 'For years we have happily patched up and repaired the existing outdated system. Now we have burst mains flooding the high street and sewage polluting the rivers.' He complained of 'underspending . . . in local authorities . . . to the tune of £1.5 billion in one year'. Under the Oxford High Street repairs were required for five weeks in 1981 to a rotting ancient sewer. The sewer is 15 feet under the surface of the High Street, and sewage was again filtering through the ground in 1983. In Farnham, Surrey, in 1985, a 'hundred year old surface water sewer' has now to be urgently replaced in the main street, at considerable local weekend inconvenience. Total chaos reigns there on a Saturday, as I write. The cost of replacing Victorian sewers would in the end be much less than that of having continuously to repair them, while traffic, trade, commerce all suffer. There is such a thing as 'the vandalism of governmental neglect'. The nation suffers, and will suffer more as time goes on, and little is done except to execute urgent repairs. Michael Hawkins, county engineer of Devon, said in his presidential address to the Institution of Municipal Engineers in 1982:

There are over 146,000 miles of public sewers in the United Kingdom, much of which was laid down by the Victorians, yet the present sewer system is decaying rapidly and has reached the point where many parts have collapsed and have been replaced, while miles of sewers are of an unknown condition, but highly suspect due to their age alone. The public health aspects cannot be over-estimated nor can the dangers from damaged sewers.[11]

A House of Lords Select Committee report on the sewers and water mains tells us that 15 percent of the sewers are more than 100 years old, that there are 5,000 sewer failures a year, and that the industry should be spending £105 million more on the system each year in order to maintain it at least in its present state. As for the water mains, 70 to 80 percent of them are of unlined cast iron, and the corrosion process is causing a progressive reduction of the pipes' ability to withstand stress. There is likely to be increased 'burst frequency' and the consequent need for complete replacement.[12]

There are other horrifying realities. Here is one involving considerable inhumanity to those incapable of resistance. Our Victorian prisons are in some cases in a state of chronic decay. HM Prison Gloucester, according to a Home Office civil servant before the House of Commons Home Affairs Committee in February 1982, suffers from gross over-crowding of cells designed for one person. It has a hospital which constitutes a health hazard, an unhygenic kitchen and inadequate fire precautions.[13] This is a terrible indictment. In Strangeways Gaol in Bury New Road, Manchester, when I visited it recently, 1,600 men and youths, many of them on remand, were being held in accommodation intended for 876. In December 1982, John McCarthy, Governor of Wormwood Scrubs, resigned from the prison service in protest. He had in 1981 denounced prison conditions as 'uncivilized and immoral' and had described prisons as 'over-crowded cattle pens'. He was regarded as a governor of considerable experience and rare skills. He had come to think of the British prison system as 'a society that debases'.[14] Efforts towards humanization in the prisons are being made. Let them be made quickly. It is good to learn in 1985 that sixteen new prisons are to be built. There are 47,000 persons in prison.

When we plead for construction and reconstruction works which will repair national damage, add to national wealth, increase productivity and reduce costs, we are asking for work to be done which will absorb unskilled and semi-skilled labour. The majority of the male unemployed are in fact unskilled and semi-skilled workers. Work which would suit them cries out to be done. I know that to have the need for work and to have the unemployed available is not enough. It is also necessary to avoid acute and prolonged inflation such as will lead to further unemployment. Giles Merritt makes very strongly the point that others have made: investment programmes do not necessarily produce inflation. He makes the clear distinction between two projects which will absorb labour, two sorts of job creation. In one a power station is built, in the other the beaches are cleared. In the building of the power station (which will serve industry and enable it to function less expensively) sub-contracts go out into large areas of the private sector. He quotes German analysis that in house-building, 'the construction industry's share of the cost of a house is only 32 percent, with the remaining 68 percent accounted for directly in sub-contracts.[15] He is proposing the sort of construction which will boost the whole economy and, it is hoped, cheapen its products.

The Scottish Bankers Magazine both warned and encouraged:

> If new forms of employment are offered more people will be employed, which will increase our national wealth; the notion that we shall ruin ourselves financially is rubbish. It must be appreciated that economic recovery requires the good will, courage and imagination of the British people. Economic policies must be mutually supportive with demand expansion being directly lined to an appropriate exchange rate and incomes policy.

The same article had already said:

> There must be a policy of national consensus involving the Government, employers and trade unions to determine how increased output is to be shared in the community. All parties to wage bargaining must be made to realize that wage rises in excess of productivity improvements merely force up prices and/or reduce real profits; the latter results in declining investment and rising unemployment.[16]

One further point must be made. It is that there is immense unemployed capacity in the economy, machinery which is not being adequately used. Indeed, manufacturing in Britain in the

1980s is wallowing in spare capacity. Dr Jim Taylor, of Lancaster University, has written very convincingly of the dangers of not using manufacturing capacity. Under-utilization of capital equipment means that it will not be replaced. British industry will become increasingly non-competitive in world markets. As existing capital becomes obsolete, unemployment grows.[17] It is a vicious circle. In the meantime, as the television shows us, some of the robots in Japan work on throughout the night with only one person to supervise them. When all the spare capacity of which Dr Taylor writes is duly used, the expansion of production would lower the cost.

A report by 'Cambridge Econometrics' claims that the Government ought to build new houses and undertake 'civil works'. It says that an expanded programme for the construction industry would do more for Britain than tax deductions or than spending money in other ways.[18] While it seems that there is much construction work that needs to be done in Britain and that the tools are available, the construction industry itself has been in a serious state of decline since 1973. We have seen earlier in this chapter the dimension in manpower of this decline. The tragic figures quoted for a country in need both of reconstruction and of work for the unemployed do not include the quarter million workers probably unemployed in the building materials and construction equipment industries.

In our continuing efforts needed to improve production and to lower costs, we need an educated work force and men and women who have benefited from tertiary education. We need more and improved university education, better training for the benefit both of the person and of the nation of those capable of tertiary education. John Wellens, with his considerable experience of the needs of industry, is convinced that revival of British industry must come from the top, from better trained managers, more high-level technologists and technicians. 'If the high level problem were to be solved,' he writes, 'the low level problem would be cured in the natural process of improving performance at the top.'[19]

There is truth in what Mr Wellens says. Yet good leadership at the top is not enough. We need a thoughtful nation, a thinking electorate, an educated work-force, if we, now a second-class power, are to deal with the formidable problems which confront us, including mass unemployment. Our school educational system is not good enough. We produce the football hooligans in large numbers, the rioters and the vandals in smaller ones. We produce school-leavers who feel strongly and reason badly, whose limited rationality tends to be dominated by their emotions. We need to educate in such a way that young people may be taught to use their reasoning capacity to the full and to attach more significance to what their reason tells them than to what they feel. That means educating them in smaller classes where highly trained teachers help to teach them to speak and to write rationally. We shall see in the next chapter how important it is to be able to express oneself verbally if one is to think clearly and logically. At a time when hundreds of thousands of young people seem doomed to unemployment, it is vital that they should learn to read, to speak, to write, so that they are not the victims of their own feelings of frustration if not of despair. All this calls for the spending of more money on secondary education. The products of large classes are often left with a consciousness of intellectual inadequacy which causes them to turn to the violent rather than to the constructive in face of human need. Violence bursts out of frustration. From good education in the end the whole nation benefits.

How is the meeting of all these national needs, full employment, construction, education, to be paid for? I have tried already to suggest that payment for national reconstruction does not necessarily involve inflation. For the financial year 1984-5, payments made necessary to State industries for losses resulting from the miners' strike amount to more than £4,000 million. These payments have had to be made to the Coal Board, to British Steel, to British Rail and to the Central Electricity Generating Board.[20] They have not generated inflation to any considerabe extent.

In the last chapter, I shall suggest a drastic and perhaps sacrificial way of meeting some of these needs, if ways involving less self-sacrifice are not tried or do not work. Let us, however, look now at these less heroic ways. The meeting of the various national needs, including full employment, ought not to depend upon the pressures which interested bodies can bring to bear upon politicians. The meeting of such needs ought to be the subject of the most careful, thorough and objective research. It is this kind of national research which this country seems to lack. Mr Geoffrey Chandler, of the National Economic Development Office, complained on 20 October, 1982, that 'the mechanisms for industrial planning simply do not exist in Britain'. In Japan and in France (with its 'Commissariat au Plan'), there is the mechanism for research and planning that Britain needs. Mr Chandler pleads for the positive 'rebuilding of British industry and its competitiveness'.[21]

Politically, there are signs that there is a consensus among party politicians of all parties who are not completely committed to a rigid party line that there is need for some measure of ordered reflation. This view is shared by the Confederation of British Industry. If there is to be some carefully researched and ordered reflation to increase national productivity and efficiency and to absorb many of the unemployed, there will inevitably follow reductions in the cost of unemployment benefit and social security payments. It is commonly said that the cost of employing a person on new work would be one and a half times the cost of paying him to be unemployed. In an Institute of Fiscal Studies paper in 1981, the researchers Mick Morris and Andrew Dilmot claimed that the cost of maintaining the unemployed was nearly £13 billion, considerably higher than Treasury estimates. The same researchers indicated that 92 percent of government spending on the unemployed is for unemployment and supplementary benefits, 8 percent for rent and rate rebates and for free school meals and welfare milk.[22] A report to the Commons Select Committee on the Social Services stated in 1981 that it then cost the taxpayer £500 a month to maintain a married man with two children. This figure has been generally accepted in Parliament, but has been challenged as too low. There would certainly be great economies in national expenditure if considerable numbers of the unemployed were removed by reflation from the unemployed register.

I listened some time ago to Sir Richard O'Brien, formerly Director of the Manpower Services Commission, speaking with great, almost unchallengable authority, at the end of a long debate on work and unemployment. Unemployment, he said, was in fact unacceptable. He explained that we were suffering not from a work crisis, but from 'an organization crisis'. To this organization crisis, he explained, as a nation we had not risen. He told us that the basis of the peculiarly national element in this crisis lay in the lack of investment compared with the amount of money that is being spent on consumption. He said that there would be no sustained growth in the economy until there was a change in investment policy. He said that for this to be effective there must be a national incomes policy. He went on to say that we must face up to high taxation if we were to cure unemployment. Relatively high taxation is necessary for a civilized society, he told us. Among a large audience of City of London men and women, none of us was able to answer him. He carried, from his intellectual status and from his experience, conviction. In a letter to *The Times* on 7th January, 1983, he wrote that 'the waste of resources involved in high unemployment, let alone the moral questions involved, demands that we consider afresh how to run the economy at a higher level of activity and thus begin the long, hard task of reducing unemployment'.[23]

I am aware that some unemployment is bound always to exist in a market economy. There must be some seasonal unemployment, for example in agriculture, in building, in tourism. Men and women change their jobs, industries inevitably decline and new ones develop even in a healthy economy. There are changes in taste, and national industries are hit by foreign competition. All this is inevitable. But it is that unemployment which goes steadily on, which seems to have no end to it, which disheartens and demoralizes, which has to be tackled and cured by the nation for the nation's sake. I am appealing for serious research, serious consideration for any schemes that may give jobs to the unemployed and at the same time benefit the community. The Labour Editor of *The Observer* writes of the unemployed that 'a civilized society has to act to help these people'. That is a moral imperative. He adds ruefully, however, that Britain 'remains a rather callous, uncaring country, where the real victims of the recession go unheard'.[24] Perhaps it is that we are sceptical of quack remedies, rather than callous. The 'real victims of the recession' (of whom he writes) go unheard, because up to now they tend to be isolated in their depression and their poverty (until suddenly here and there among the young, the rioting begins). Unemployment at present isolates much more than it unites. There is for the unemployed no community; the unemployed tend to keep to themselves. An American Jesuit comments, 'When a person is no longer related to other persons, he is quite literally dead'.[25] It is from this living death that society must raise the unemployed.

NOTES

1 *National Westminster Bank Quarterly Review*, February 1985, p. 31.

2 *New Statesman*, February 1982, p. 5.

3 *New Technology Case Studies*, T.U.C., 1980, p. 1.

4 *New Technology and Employment*, M.S.C., 1982, paras. 1, 2, 3, 4, 6.

5 *Science, Technology and Public Policy*, No. 1, University of Sussex, 1982, pp. 4, 7.

6 C. Johnson, Group Economics Adviser, Lloyds Bank, *The Times*, 20 January 1982, p.10.

7 *Crisis in Construction*, National and Local Government Officers Association, pp. 33, 39.

8 *The Guardian*, 15 August 1982, p. 3.

9 *World out of Work*, Collins, 1982, p. 184.

10 ibid., p. 181.

11 *Water Bulletin*, 18 June 1982, p. 3.

12 *Water*, September 1981, p. 8.

13 *The Guardian*, 18 February 1982, p. 14.

14 ibid., 3 December 1982, p. 1.

15 *World out of Work (op.cit.)*, pp. 177, 179.

16 February 1982, pp. 137, 136.

17 *Productive Potential in the U.K. Manufacturing Sector*, University of Lancaster, December 1981, p. 21.

18 *Policies for Recovery*, Cambridge Econometrics, 1981, pp. 12-13.

19 *Industrial and Commercial Training*, July 1981, p. 219.

20 *Daily Telegraph*, 15 February 1985, p. 4.

21 *The Guardian*, 16 October 1981, p. 26.

22 *Scottish Bankers Magazine*, November 1981, p. 88.

23 p. 9.

24 31 January, 1982, p. 8.

25 R. A. McCormick: *How Brave a New World? (op.cit.)*, p. 14.

9

Unhappiness at Work

My theme is that unemployment is damaging to all who suffer it.
This is because a person fulfils, completes himself in his work. He
is unfulfilled without it. However, some will inevitably point out
that for some workers their work is frustrating, unsatisfying.
They are not fulfilled by it. That is, of course, true. I propose in
this chapter to try to show how in some cases work is not
fulfilling, and to consider how those frustrations and other causes
of industrial conflict can be eliminated. I believe that most serious
industrial disputes can be avoided. I believe that far more and
better training of management and workers could make them
quite unnecessary. I believe also that such training could
supplement people's mostly inadequate education in economics
and psychology and sociology and could also help all concerned to
appreciate the needs of the unemployed. It is not good enough to
say that the problems are primarily moral; they are also
intellectual; people will not even try to do what is right until they
learn what it is right to do. I believe that we need a better
educated and more thoughtful work force (including both 'sides'
of industry), and that the unemployed will in fact benefit from the
kind of training of those in work that helps them to understand
human need as a whole.

The Scottish Bankers Magazine, in a long article by J. Leslie of
the Department of Accountancy and Finance at Heriot-Watt
University, told us in November 1981 something of what the
author believed to be wrong with our industry:

> The U.K. economy suffers from severe long-term structural problems –
> low productivity, poor labour relations; inadequate investment and bad
> management – to outside observers our country also appears to suffer from
> deep divisive social problems and a lack of common purpose. Between
> 1973-78 U.K. manufacturing productivity grew by 0.5 percent per
> annum, compared with an annual increase of 1.3 percent, 3.9 percent and
> 5.9 percent for the U.S.A., Germany and Japan respectively. These
> figures highlight the real problems in our manufacturing industry, i.e. low
> output per worker.

In 1979 the trade unions rejected wage restraint; the earnings index rose by 15½ percent, followed by 20½ percent in 1980. As a result, the UK inflation rate was well above our foreign competitors, and this, combined with low productivity, made our exports uncompetitive. In 1980/81 the UK manufacturing sector experienced a severe contraction in output and employment; the trade unions cannot shift the entire blame for rising unemployment onto the Conservative Government's economic policy. . . .

Whatever the reader's political leanings, it must be obvious that the price of labour in relation to its output is a crucial factor in determining the level of unemployment. Yet, some trade unions demand wage increases which, when granted, put some of their own members out of work and thereby increase total unemployment in the economy. A key condition for the maintenance of full employment is wage moderation. This was identified by Beveridge in the mid-1940s.[1]

Since this was written, labour productivity in British manufacturing industry has risen by 17 percent. It could rise higher, given better industrial relationships. Out of its rise could come employment rather than unemployment. I believe in the possibilities of training and have found on both management and shop steward courses open-mindedness, reasonableness, and a will to learn that has surprised me. I believe that when really good training is made more available on both sides of industry, there will be not only better understanding and relationships within it, but an increase of understanding of and care for the plight of those excluded from it by unemployment. In addition, the better understanding by both sides of the economic, psychological and sociological facts of life will lead to greater fellowship within industry and greater productivity. From such improvement, resulting in greater prosperity, the unemployed (among others) will be the gainers. Let me describe as best I can something of the thinking of several groups of workers with whom I have been in recent close contact. I am trying to show that not only ordinary managers but ordinary workers have reasoning capacity and moral sense. One of my unemployed friends, one of the most reasonable and most moral of them, feels very strongly that this reasonableness and this moral sense are by no means adequately portrayed on the news media.

The faces and voices of two groups whom I propose very briefly to describe are vivid to me. I have careful notes of what members of both groups said, as well as records of the results of questions to and discussions with one group. I should describe the nineteen members of the one group and the thirty-nine members of the other group as being nearly all thoughtful, almost all open to reason, none of them religiously or (except for one in the second group) politically orientated. Both groups seemed to me to represent slightly above-the-average quality among trade unionists, men (and a woman) in close touch with their less thoughtful brethren and capable of influence within their respective unions. The majority of the first (and younger) group were electricians, and the majority of the second group were coal-miners.

In the first group most of the men (and the woman) were in their middle and late twenties. In the second group most of the men were in their thirties or forties. Various characteristics were common to almost all in both groups. They were interested in their jobs; some of them even spoke openly of 'enjoying' them. They were mostly keen to do well at their jobs. They were not particularly keen to gain promotion or status, but all wanted to earn more money. They wished to be able to afford 'luxuries' such as improved housing or a car. However, in different ways they were all adamant that money earnings were not their priority. A group of the younger men declared incidentally that in negotiations financial benefit was the last thing they aimed for. This was said quietly, and agreed to without demur. The older men placed it on record with emphasis that they valued 'flexible hours of work in conformity with their needs' more highly than a big wage. Almost all agreed that they would be unhappy without work, however much money they might have. Despite the different impression of the British worker sometimes given by the news media, I formed and have maintained, a high opinion of the honesty of those who spoke in this way in both groups. I heard much the same recently in a third group (and, in 1985, in a fourth).

In the first and younger group, where the majority were shop stewards in their 20s (and early 30s), I saw and heard over and over again a keenness to learn, to know more, indeed a hunger and thirst for knowledge. They were mostly the products of the secondary modern schools, which (despite their many excellencies) had left them uneducated concerning both economics and the art of relationships. They were not only mostly politically unprejudiced; they were politically ignorant. They were responsible, but just did not honestly know what was best for themselves, for their fellow-workers and for the unemployed. School had left them both without the material to use in forming economic, financial and political decisions, and without training in the making of judgements. One young man of about twenty-five had been to two excellent shop stewards' training courses in one year in an attempt to equip himself for his job. He was growing all the time in mental stature, but was still very conscious of his ignorance.

In the second and larger group (of mostly older men from the North) a very few had obviously come to the conclusion that their days for serious thinking were over. As I have said, only one could be described as politically prejudiced (in the sense that his mind was made up as to what was to blame for whatever was wrong). The rest included some youngish and early middle-aged men who were natural leaders: trade union officials, trade union representatives, magistrates, councillors. Like some of those in the younger group, there was a minority amongst them of some intellectual status, men who grasped and remembered whatever they heard, although they did not read very much. Such men would have risen high in management if they had been given the chance and had cared to go over to 'the other side'. I asked one outstanding man if he had ever been given that chance. He said in reply that he had just once been offered it. Of course, he had turned it down. He was a union man; divisions and non-relationships are too great in much of industry for union men to accept such offers. So capacity for managemental skills tends to be unused. A considerable number of this thoughtful and mature group confessed that they were more happy in their working hours than in their non-working hours. This was a confession which would not of course, be made in public or in the presence of 'the other side'. Except where real trust has been created in industrial relations, there is inevitably an element of play-acting between the two sides. This was freely admitted. One of the group added that you had to remember that they were members of 'a close-knit community who enjoyed one another's company'. Very quietly and without any rhetoric, a group within the group (with which I myself as its reporter was involved) expressed conviction of the need to replace the profit motive. All agreed that they would greatly appreciate a four day working week. We shall see in the last chapter something of the case for the shorter working week. There was far more to the thinking and speaking of this group of balanced and competent men than wages and hours and conditions of work. There was considerable thought expressed for the conservation and development of resources. There was great distrust of control from London. There was agreement that the regions, where resources could be best appreciated and needs most clearly seen, were the places from which funds for development could best be distributed. They felt for the unemployed, but had not thought sufficiently deeply. Let me emphasize that here in these two groups, amongst these men (and the woman) were persons ripe for further education, persons capable of learning and of hard thinking, capable of co-operation for the benefit of production, the sort of persons whom British industry and community ought to use to the full. They were persons who deserve the best training that the trade unions can give or that the companies can give (in so far as the companies can be trusted to make that training objective and non-manipulative).

There are, however, obstacles in the way of creating a thoughtful, co-operative workforce, which cause the workers sometimes to seek confrontation and conflict instead of education and co-operation. Take Howard. He is a skilled craftsman, in his early forties. He has worked for a scaffolding company for more than twenty years. He would like to get out. He has had enough of it. He has his opinions, founded on experience. He is not asked for these opinions. If he gives them, he is told by management to 'leave it to me'. He leaves it, and nothing is done. He is obviously tired of 'hanging about'. He is sent off to Stourbridge to do a job. He gets there at 8.30 for 9am, and no one in management turns up till 11.30. He asks if accommodation has been booked for the night. He is told that it has been; but in fact it is not booked until 4pm. Then it is in a pub in process of reconstruction. There is no hot water and there are no meals. He has a meal out, and there is considerable argument concerning the paying of the bill. He is tired of it all. 'Management won't listen,' he says. He repeats with a look of hopelessness, 'Management won't listen'. Twenty years ago, he says, it was different. Now, he says, management thinks more of profits than of people. He does not say what we all know: that profits depend upon people. He could go over to management, he says, but then he would miss out on his over-time. He needs his over-time to live, he says.

Discount Howard's story, if you like, as that of a decent but disgruntled man. However, there are thousands (and hundreds of thousands) who could tell the same tale. If workers need educational training and need it badly, so too does management, especially in the psychology of the worker. Management receives training; but sometimes it is not the right kind of training. I was present at a supervisors' training course, where, somehow or other, the message did not get across at all (except to a very small group gathered immediately around the tutor). I am pleading for the very best kind of training, at whatever cost, for training which it will pay Government to subsidize most generously, because it will be the key to better relationships within industry and to higher productivity. If it helps people to look at the needs and welfare of the whole community, it may help to produce a new attitude to the deprived, the unemployed.

Let us take another look at Tony, now (in 1985), sadly departed from us. Here, it seems to me, is the British worker, disappointed in shop floor relationships, and yet with that vision that enables him to work for a cause. After twenty-three years Tony chose to leave 'Cambridge Exhausts'. He said that he felt that conditions had deteriorated, that there was 'a general feeling of futility'. He did not care to think of his doing another eighteen years there in an atmosphere like that. He could not face it. 'I'm told since', he said, 'that it's worsened'. He was referring to what seemed to be a new type of management, one, he said, that just did not seem to care. 'It didn't seem to be concerned,' he told me. It seemed to him to be a change from management by engineers to management by accountants. Now, he said, they sat in offices working over figures. He called the old General Manager a tyrant. However, he added that he would walk through every shop every morning and that he would know just what was going on. He was respected. He told the story of the new General Manager who picked up an aluminium bracket and asked if it was plated or stainless. He said that the worker who was making it (for Citroen) 'nearly died of shock'. He just could not believe his ears. How could someone high in management be as ignorant as all that? Tony said that this was where we had failed badly. 'Management', he said, 'just does not seem concerned about a totally good product'. He said that he watched this process going on during his last year at Exhausts. He explained that the basis of management is man-management; he added that there just had to be mutual respect. He had watched respect for management die away. He said that 'there is simply no substitute for good man-management'. He explained that at one time the General Manager would select a foreman from the production line. Now a foreman would come from the tool-makers or the fitters. He just would not know the job on the production line. He said that if he himself had stayed on, all this change of management style could have damaged him. He could have become a cabbage. Now, he said, he was glad to be out of that factory where management and workers had lost touch and mutual respect. Contact had gone, respect had gone, trust had gone. With the going of all that, he went himself. He was a man of both character and integrity. He went into football promotion because he could put his heart into it. He spent most of his spare time assisting with boys' football. He had a vision and a sense of vocation concerning the importance of decent lads keeping fit and learning sportsmanship.

Workers are sometimes presented in the news media as concerned only with their own financial gain. They are often guilty of selfishness, but they are also capable of altruism. There is sometimes a shrugging of shoulders concerning other people's difficulties, concerning for example the lot of the unemployed. This is not because they do not care but because they do not know what to do about it. They need the maximum of adult education, such as could be made possible for them on training courses. For management, as well as for workers, training courses provide marvellous opportunities for learning and growth. On courses, I have seen young managers (and some not so young), young supervisors, and many shop stewards really keen to remedy their ignorance, to listen, to discuss wisely, to learn. On an E.E.T.P.U. 'intermediate' shop stewards' course at Cudham Hall, I have heard teaching which was objective, fearlessly clear, and very well received by young men (and some not so young) who showed themselves unprejudiced, and willing to learn. I believe that if faith in such courses were to develop, we should find more and more men and women within industry not only learning how to work together but also developing a sense of a larger community and of obligation within that community.

Both managers and unions sometimes demonstrate ignorance concerning the sort of training that each party needs. Management in places suffers from the traditional idea that 'leaders are born not made'. This is the tradition of the successful gifted amateur. In my *Justice in Industry* I record how I inquired from one high authority whether his managers were trained. I was told that 'our managers have degrees'. A degree in accountancy or economics does not ensure capacity to manage people. It is true that training may sometimes be of the wrong kind. Sometimes management training is provided as a ritual act, to satisfy modern canons of management. That is not good enough. If good training is not rigorously sought and sedulously pursued, the training will be poor in quality. It may then be logical for the trainee to return to his job to be told (as the Australian put it in my quotation in *Justice in Industry*): 'So now you've been on a fancy human relations course. Get out there and kick arses.'[2] The same Australian author has a long chapter on 'The Gap between Saying and Doing'.[3] In Nichols and Beynon's *Living with Capitalism*,[4] the sociologists describe lack of practical managemental human concern in a chemicals plant whose top management is in theory dedicated to the best sort of concern for relationships. Something had gone wrong. As all members of management ought to learn to be concerned with the efficiency of the business (whether it be publicly or privately owned), so ought all to be concerned with the understanding and respect due to the workers and with the human and business need to 'involve' them to the full. The conversion of mind and will which all this entails would be better coming from individual conviction; but if it does not come this way it is up to top management to make sure that it comes from steady and sustained pressure on all ranks of management. If top management and leaders of trade unions are beginning to realize how connected their own welfare is with the well-being of the nation, they will see to it that on training courses men and women are helped to understand in what that well-being consists and how best it can be promoted.

Let us look in more detail first at management training and then at the training of shop stewards. The industrial situation itself, as well as the situation of the nation, cries out for more and better management training. We have to try to convince top management of the truth of this. Sheena Crane, after considerable experience of management training, writes that one of the most difficult problems is to gain a real commitment to training from senior management. She tells of the collapse of some excellent schemes of training because of lack of managemental support. She speaks of 'a complex mixture of psychological, social, economic and financial attitudes' on management's part which sometimes makes the task of the trainer difficult. She describes how she sometimes has to search amongst management for one person really committed to training, for one person in senior management who understands the importance of it. She has become used to the traditional objections: 'There are better things to spend your money on . . . We've never needed training in the past . . . Train people and they leave.'[5] Sometimes, there is in management a cock-sureness, a sense of not needing to learn anything, perhaps acquired at school, perhaps veiling a fear of being shown up. Sometimes, there is a reserve or a shyness or a fear of accepting reasoned criticism. 'When I was a manager, I thought I knew all there was to be known about it,' says one who now regrets that attitude. Somehow good training has to be brought in, partially at least to help those who think and talk like that. A National Economic Development Office report declared that the main causes of certain problems were 'insensitive management, complex pay schemes and the basic boredom of mass production'.[6] Sensitive management, well trained management, would not have needed a report from outside to discover such causes.

Gerry Hutton, an Associate Adviser of the Industrial Society, long concerned with training in a famous Lancashire engineering firm, was for a considerable period given responsibility for its training of managers, foremen, charge-hands and shop stewards. He had first of all to make sure that everyone throughout the firm and its subsidiaries had a personal interview with 'the boss' immediately above him. It was strangely difficult to achieve this. Some bosses simply did not understand that the persons who worked for them would appreciate a little personal interest. Once people did understand that the boss was taking a personal interest, they were prepared to be told that 'the firm would like to send them on a course'. Each person's agreement was needed; it would have to be made clear to him as well as to his boss that the course was suitable for him. All this may sound trivial to some;

but it is based upon what people are and how they feel. If the family and the school had been the training ground for relationships that they sometimes claim to be, there would not be all this need for further training. In fact people go into life and work all too often unprepared for close contact with those with whom they will have to live and work. They do not know how to treat their next door neighbour because they have lived isolated from him. The good training course should help them not only in how to behave to those above them and below them and alongside them at work, but also in how to look out in understanding and care towards the community outside upon whom they in some measure depend. If those in authority (and down the management line) could realize the importance of training for relationships, there would be a real step forward in responsible industrial relations and in a responsible attitude towards problems of the community such as unemployment.

If managers are to learn how to manage men and women, they have to learn on training courses to look at themselves and to hear themselves. They have to see their own faces when they are worried or angry, to hear their own voices when they are in a hurry. They have to be ready to be told what they really look like and sound like, to be hurt, and to recover from the hurting. They have to be helped to look back and see how early in life they developed that authoritarian look or tone, that hasty temper with which to attempt to settle matters. They have to learn that such habits which were unconsciously picked up can be consciously dispensed with. All this belongs to the good training course. Training and the realization of the need for training can fade out, given the human failings of all concerned. John Wellens of *Industrial and Commercial Training* is almost brutally realistic about this. He pleads for a 'conversion', a real change of mind and will, a reasoned determination on the part of management to work with the workers. He helps us to realize that we are to seek something which belongs, whether we know it or not, to the ethics of the Christian religion: the determination to treat our fellow human beings justly. To secure this justice, we need training conducted with conviction, devotion and zeal. I myself have been allowed the privilege of attending two quite different sorts of management training courses. In both cases, the person primarily responsible was himself well-trained and thoroughly competent. Yet in one case I felt strongly that more obvious conviction, more signs of conversion on the part of the trainer were needed. I expect the conversion was there; but it did not sufficiently show. In the other case, it must have been plain to all that a considerable number of the trainees were not really interested and were really just waiting for the pubs to open. The trainer was up against utter lack of conversion, of willingness even to consider the possibility of conversion. In *Industrial and Commercial Training*, Donald Wright, of the Education and Training Department of the Trustee Savings Bank, wrote:

> Most trainees leave Training Centres with new ideas and skills and a determination to apply these skills on their return to the work situation. Unfortunately, on return to real life the trainee, in addition to the comments of 'forget what you learned at the Training Centre . . . this is how we do it here', has to face the fact that theory and practice are poles apart, that 'the Organization' is all powerful, that management and worker perceptions are difficult, if not impossible, to change in the short or medium term.[7]

John Wellens pleads and threatens: 'What is required is a new style of work organisation and administration which is adopted out of conviction that it is the best way of ordering human relationships and the best way of creating wealth and producing those material goods which make up our standard of living. It can be described as the joint-problem-solving or joint-decision-making style. . . . My thesis is that this style of management is crucial to our success in the immediate future. This is the starting point of the long road to resurgence or prosperity in the circumstances of tomorrow's world.'[8] In other words, the conversion to justice within industry and within the community, and to the determined and persistent training for it has to begin at the top of the industry and to be pursued rigorously all the way down the management line.[9]

Real conversion of management, a lasting, persevering determination to secure the best and most fearless training possible, is part of the process by which trust is to be won. A mere flash-in-the-pan, short-life commitment to training will not do. I have in mind a building in the midst of a large plant; it was the training centre of a great industrial enterprise. It is used now for other purposes. There seems to the workers in recent years to have been a hardening of middle management and supervisory attitudes in that place, a sense that the workers must just learn 'to take it'. Language is bad about the workers and towards the workers. It is proclaimed that this is the language they can best understand. 'Those training fellows' are not needed any more. The attitude is 'I'm the boss and you can take it'. There has been promotion from the shop floor. Those who were sworn at on the shop floor now swear at their successors there. In the past managers would be often on the shop floor to show workers how best to do a job. They swore, but there was respect. Now there is much more swearing, much less respect. Mutual respect has gone. No one seems to think how (or whether) it could be won back. In such an atmosphere, there develop inevitably wearing tensions. Those divided inside have little care for the total welfare of their own community, let alone for the greater community outside. People's capacity for altruism is lessened by internal contempt, suspicion, warfare.

Let me move on to the all-important subject of the training of shop stewards. Here are the men and women who are trusted by their fellow-workers to represent them. Many of the older ones are content as they are; some are too domestically over-burdened to be of much service to their electorate. Amongst the majority of the younger ones there is often a keenness to learn, to equip themselves for their jobs, combined with a sometimes painful sense of their own ignorance, their lack of the right kind of education. The T.U.C. organizes courses, and some individual unions provide them. It is generally agreed that some of the T.U.C. courses are dull and uninspiring. It is easier to educate in industrial law than in industrial relations. Shop stewards, leaders amongst the workers on the shop floor, need to learn something about economics. The subject ought to be well taught. They need to learn something concerning the springs of human behaviour. Call it psychology, if you like. Despite Department of Education and Science support, the T.U.C. has not a vast amount of money available for the payment (and expenses) of teachers. The Jim Conway Foundation is a first-rate research and training institution for trade unionists. It attracts to its courses mature trade union men and women of experience and thoughtfulness. During one year, its twenty-two educational projects involved nearly a thousand trade union men and women and keen youngsters, some in work and some in unemployment. It also has a first-rate Research Department available for its members. At one of its week-end seminars, it was agreed that, while T.U.C. courses for shop stewards 'were useful, there were deficiencies'. 'Not sufficient was being done to educate union representatives'. Its Research Officer suggested that 'release courses might be a useful basis for trade union education'. The delegates were of one mind that the trade unions had representatives with great ability but that they needed better education to equip them to deal with the complex problems now facing the unions. 'As a long term policy trade union education facilities must be expanded.'[10] They could not have been more right. Quite apart from older persons, young people glad enough to leave school at sixteen frequently find themselves ready for further education in their twenties. Good training courses help to minister to this newly-discovered need. Investment by employers and by Governments in this very real kind of education, provided that no strings are attached, would be of inestimable value for British industry and for the welfare of the whole community. There is on the part of many shop stewards, including older ones who have reached positions of considerable authority, an ill-concealed and deep sense of inferiority. This sometimes results in unworthy behaviour born of frustration; only the maximum of the best of training can begin to remedy this.

If amongst British workers we are to develop shop stewards (and others) committed not only to their own industry but to the welfare of the community, there has to be a new and listening and trusting attitude to the workers. My friend, John F. Hird, Senior Staff Engineer at the Baltimore, Maryland Works of the Western Electric Company, writes some sound advice concerning objectives for a programme of 'participative management'. He urges that such a programme must be a 'continuing' one, 'to establish a commonality of interest, mutual trust, and interdependence between hourly and salaried employees and technical and nontechnical supervisors at all levels of management'. He asks for the removal of 'restrictive conditions which inhibit employees' self-development and growth on the job'. He pleads for the making available to all employees of 'voluntary training in group dynamics, social therapy, work simplification, value engineering, and quality control techniques'.[11] This is American phraseology; but my personal experience of the author and of the esteem in which he is held in industrial circles in the eastern United States leads me to maintain strongly my belief that he writes what he knows by experience.

Industry needs men and women who believe that at work they matter and yet who are aware that they have to go on learning as they work, and that their own future depends upon co-operation with others. They need security, a sense of community; they need to feel that they are understood and even cared for. British industry needs workers devoted to their work, and the community needs members who have learnt to look out with interest and care from secure and well-paid jobs to the needs of others less fortunate. John Wellens wrote in 1981-2 some challenging articles called 'Operation Phoenix', concerning 'living and working in a technological society'. He can scarcely be branded as 'an activist' or 'a man of the left'. He believes in the capacity and the specific duty of management to produce a solution of the present impasse in industrial relations. In the past, he believes it has been through its management of men that society has worked out its salvation. He writes that in 'yesterday's world . . . people counted for very little'. 'They were', he says, 'servants of the machine . . . hands, they were called.' He goes on to say that this world was 'authoritarian, harsh and insensitive to people and their needs'. He says (surprisingly) that this tradition lasted until long after the end of World War 2. He says (as if he means it) that 'tomorrow's world must be a world in which people matter', that there must be joint problem-solving, with workers involved fully in that task. He suggests that the 'Quality Circle' problem-solving approach may prove suitable for much of British industry.[12]

I saw Quality Circles in operation at Wedgwoods at Barlaston. I was not in the least prepared for the keenness, indeed the dedication, of which I saw the signs among the workers whom I met there who belonged to the Quality Circles. When I first went to Wedgwoods, Quality Circles had been operating there for two years. They have been developing, changing, improving there all the time. In the words of one worker, they have become 'more and more a way of life'. Usually eight persons meet in a Circle, all from the same work area, and they receive eight one hour periods of training. Sometimes a Circle in operation consists of only six people, sometimes even of only three. They have their own training and operating area at Wedgwoods. Dick Fletcher, the 'general facilitator' until April 1985, is inclined to think that eight is too many for a Circle after the initial training period. He himself was the leader at Wedgwoods of a team of eight 'facilitators' (or coordinators). The original chosen leaders of Circles were foremen or forewomen or chargehands. At the end of the training period, the Circles were ready to analyse what was wrong or inadequate in the work they were doing, to work out a solution or improvement, and to 'present' their conclusions and recommendations to management. Management, sometimes even senior management, attended the presentation. Recommendations were, believe it or not, acted on. Specks were made to disappear from pottery, new brushes recommended, designed, ordered, new boxes which were needed were produced. Wedgwood Circles tackle all sorts of projects in their area: 'Productivity, Quality, Reduction of Scrap, Quality of Life and also Environmental Improvements'. They request visits from suppliers in order to ensure that materials and tools are exactly what they want. Circles visit manufacturers' factories to see articles being made, so that they can discuss at first hand what they need. If the manufacturer happens to have adopted the Quality Circle approach to working life, then so much the better, because immediately there is common ground.

Quality Circles often combine together to solve joint or related problems, not forgetting also that each department in production is the immediate customer of the one before. Circles are therefore encouraged to make or repeat presentations to the other members of their department or associated departments. Circles are also in constant demand to make presentations at Works Council Meetings or to visiting dignatories, Members of Parliament, County Council Chairmen. Two-thirds of the Circle leaders are now hourly-paid operatives. Good provision is made for meeting places for the Circles. The boss learns from the workers what is needed and why. 'Everybody meets the boss,' a worker told me with a grin. Of course, not all the workers were converted. Sometimes there were clashes of personality in the Circles. Workers joined them and left. I personally met some of those who had left. There was, of course, some prejudice against the Circles. Nevertheless, there are now 170 Circles functioning amongst the

4,000 workers at 'Wedgwood' (as they call it). There has certainly been improvement in quality of production (and of distribution, too). All seem to have benefited. Quite young and simple girls told me smilingly that Circles 'were improving things'. An older man on the shop floor said to me that 'this gives you confidence'. 'Everybody can lead,' another man told me. He adds that 'we all want to be involved'. Without the 'QCs', an older woman said to me, there would have been arguments and incriminations. I saw two small 'QCs' working things out for themselves in the Quality Circle Centre. I found myself in what seemed to me to be a new atmosphere in British industry. I had not quite seen or heard the like of it before. Each Circle meets at least weekly for an hour (or more) at a time. Here are considerable numbers of workers, and managers too, talking together freely and cheerfully about dedicated work.

I have seen similar groups of dedicated workers striving together for quality at Daimlers (for Jaguar Cars) and at Cummins Engineering (at Daventry). It would be not only for the benefit of productivity, but for the benefit of all persons engaged in the work, for as many as possible to be similarly involved together in understanding and co-operation for quality. Concentration on quality gives workers a capacity for appreciation which, given education in social virtues, may stimulate them to seek quality in society.

In the United States, according to the American Society for Training and Development, businesses and industry allocate more than $30,000,000,000 a year to the education and training of employees.[13] Of course, as the keen and efficient manager of a small business with exceptionally good relationships said to me, 'It must be the right sort of training'. It ought to be that sort of training which can already be found in places where the aim is 'conversion' towards a will for justice towards the enterprise, towards fellow-workers and towards the community. I am asking indeed for a conversion towards the welfare of our fellow human beings, including the unemployed.

The kind of programme of training which promotes respect for the personality of the worker, for the unions to which he belongs (and in which he believes), and also for the deprived, the unemployed, may sound to some as if it were politically orientated. It is so indeed, if 'politically' means that it concerns the welfare of the whole 'city', the community. However, if 'politically' means that I am advocating the policy of a political party, that is not so. Socialism in itself is no solution to the problem of unhappiness at work. Nor does it necessarily bring about new care on the part of the worker for the welfare of the whole community. Poland in 1980-1, when 'free' trade unionism was active, and Yugo-Slavia, with its peculiar style of factory management, are examples of attempts within socialism to involve the worker and to give him a sense of responsibility in his work. The U.S.S.R., on the other hand, seems to specialize in that type of bad management which disgusts the worker whose full co-operation the welfare of industry and community requires. One cannot forget the glimpses of Soviet society in *The First Circle* of that outstanding man of integrity, Alexander Solzenitsyn. He tells of 'healthy young men, chosen for their toughness', so grossly mismanaged that 'in their years of service they had forgotten how to work'. He writes:

> It was more than flesh and blood could bear to be hopelessly caught up in impossible, grotesque, crippling schedules. You were trapped and held in a deadly grip. The system crushed you, driving you harder and faster all the time, demanding more and more, setting inhuman time-limits. This was why buildings and bridges collapsed, why crops rotted in the fields or never came up at all. But until it dawned on someone that people were only human, there was no way out of this vicious circle for those involved, except by falling ill, getting caught in a machine or having some other kind of accident . . . then they could live in hospital or in a sanatorium while it all blew over.[14]

The most recent and carefully collected comments from reliable witnesses confirm all this. A letter from workers in a Togliatti dairy products combine tells a sorry story of inhumanity and mismanagement. In face of the situation, write the workers: 'We have only the right to be silent. . . . We are taught to observe the great silence.'[15]

A mechanic from the Sverdlovsk area declares that 'agriculture is mismanaged'. A Togliatti worker complains that goods simply do not get into stores. The pressure of shopping is notorious; the pressure of work is less well-known. A Ukranian mechanic from Dneprodzherzinsk complains: 'Our women age fast because they work too hard.' An unskilled woman worker of Yaroslav asks for retirement age to be reduced. 'The way things are right now', she says, 'you're dead before you can benefit from retirement'. Soviet workers have their ways of letting their opinions become known. A foreman reports that there is too much laziness and drunkenness at his place of work.[16] Human nature reacts to inhuman pressure in varied ways. Here under the Soviet form of socialism, we see illustrated the worst faults of the so-called unacceptable face of capitalism. Here is that lack of respect for the worker which causes him to become obsessed with his own misery at work, instead of being able to co-operate in fellowship and understanding and to develop care for others.

Paul Rathkey, Head of Research for the Jim Conway Foundation, claimed on 21 March 1981 that the 1980s pose many challenges to the trade union movement. The question of involvement and responsibility, he wrote, may prove to be 'one of the greats'. 'The role of participation lay at the heart of moving from a reactive and defensive attitude to a more active and positive approach.'[17] What I am pleading for is an attitude by management to workers which encourages them to give their views, based upon their experience, as rationally as they are able, knowing that those views will be given serious consideration by management. Every worker who thinks about his work ought to be encouraged to speak out, on the assumption that he will be listened to. 'Wholeness', writes Douglas Pett, formerly of St. Mary's Hospital, Praed Street, 'implies the ability and opportunity to express our deepest thoughts, and to share them with another who understands.'[18] It is 'wholeness' that we want for persons, employed and unemployed. Wholeness means the maximum use and development of human resources, so long as that is consistent with health. It means education and training, it means opportunity to listen and to be listened to. It means willingness to think; it means development of personality towards others.

As I come towards the end of this chapter, let me try to be a little more constructive, drawing even more fully on the wisdom of others. Managers, as C.B.I. Conferences show, are becoming more convinced of the need for a new style of management, for joint problem-solving with their workers. I have seen glimpses of this at work in various factories. It is good to see. Not all training courses are up-to-date, or have quite realized that the question of whether or not joint problem-solving is to be practised no longer exists among those who understand industrial relations. Joint problem-solving has to be practised. The question on which guidance from the training courses is needed is how it is to be practised. Management and its trainers have to do all they can, to learn all they can, in order that this new style of participation may become effective as soon as possible, for British industry's sake, and indeed for the whole community's sake. John Wellens writes to me: 'Managers as a whole seem to me to be aware of the need for a new style based on joint problem-solving and the need for a new relationship between managers and their subordinates. You can take this not as an issue of conflict but as a tenet of the new order. This is not, in other words where we end up, it is where we start. The issue is not the validity or the desirability of this new style but how to bring it about and how to remove the obstacles to its widespread adoption.' (22 Sept. 1982) The field is opening up: let it be fully opened. Out of it all may come a more happy relationship within the works, and (with good teaching) a more generous outlook from the work-force, perhaps even towards the unemployed.

All this represents valuable and indeed dynamic development. It calls for exceptionally good management. It calls too for a new outlook amongst the workers: a willingness to grow together for the sake of the community at work and for the community outside. I believe that many workers and the better shop stewards, their elected representatives, can see this. I see the faces as I sit here of many shop stewards, of all ages, who understand and sympathize with what I mean.

We seek on all sides the development of the balanced mind, the mind that is caring as well as wise, the mind that is wide in its sympathies as well as strong in its principles. Let us see if Hannah Arendt can help us to see more clearly. She was a distinguished Jewish German-American writer with a clear perception of human need, of the need for full development for all. Persons, she saw, ought to be helped and encouraged to learn to talk, if they are to be helped and encouraged to think. Clear expression in speech, she is saying, assists towards clear thinking. If people are to be encouraged to speak rationally, they must also be encouraged to believe that there may be at least the possibility of action as a result of their speaking. Many speak irresponsibly, talk nonsense, because they think that no one will pay attention to what they say, that all that they say will be discounted, that nothing will happen. The most pathetic message I received in my researches for *Justice in Industry* was that of the quite dedicated trade union convener concerning the equally dedicated management: 'They always listen to us and they never do anything about it.' When I heard that in that place of good men and women, my heart sank. John Wellens complains that trade unions refuse to accept responsibility for the economic health of the country. He goes on to say that this irresponsibility precludes them from claiming any say in the highest economic councils of the nation. The answer to this charge is to see that workers are involved to the maximum in local industrial decision-making, and to do all that is in the power of employers and Government to assist in the development of first-rate training for shop stewards (and other workers). Hannah Arendt is trying to teach us all that speech and action are closely linked, that speech must be seen to lead at least sometimes to action if it is to be good, reasoned speech. It is in the combination of speech and action, she says, that human uniqueness lies. This combination, she tells us, is specifically the work of man. 'Power', she says, 'is actualized only where work and deed have not parted company, where words are not empty and deeds not brutal, where words are not used to veil intentions but to disclose realities, and deeds not used to violate and destroy, but to establish relations and create new realities.' She goes on: 'Power springs up between men when they act together and vanishes the moment they disperse. . . . Only where men live so close together that the potentialities of action are always present can power remain with them . . . whoever, for whatever reasons, isolates himself and does not partake in such being together, forfeits power and becomes impotent, no matter how great his strength and how valid his reasons.'[19] From top management to the toilet cleaner, persons in industry must find time and opportunity and words with which to talk to one another, however limited the time or clumsy the tongue, and on the implicit understanding that what is said by the humblest may lead to action by the greatest.

The more I have seen of 'late-developers' (such as those who have taken A-levels and gained good degrees in their late twenties or early thirties), the more dissatisfied I have become with

English schooling, and the more important to me has become education and training for all ranks in industry. Neil Warren, A.U.E.W. convener at Falmouth Shiprepair and secretary of the Joint Negotiating Committee there, tells me of how the very best that the work force has to give is brought out in that shipyard. 'All possible information to the men at all times is given,' he says. He speaks of 'negotiations of every sort taking place between management, men and shop stewards who know and trust one another'. The same people meet again and again, he says, co-opting others as required for different purposes. 'Total involvement', he said, 'makes for keen interested workers'. He knows what he is talking about. He adds that you get sensible responses if you give full explanations of problems. He speaks of 'union willingness to modify rules in the interest of economic operation'. All this is within the 'closed shop'. He says (as if he means it) that 'our first priority is towards the customer'. It seems that at Falmouth thoughtful co-operation has paid. The small company purchased by P and O in 1973 at that time employed approximately 1600 persons. Until ship-building nationalisation in 1977, numbers at work declined; and finally in 1979, 1106 persons were made redundant. From that sad time, with a work force of only 175, new management and new union policies began to create 'different methods and attitudes'. A loss of £3,500,000 was changed into a profit of nearly £1,000,000. The work force rose to 450. This was in 1983. All had learnt from one another. People who learn to 'look after' one another for the common good are people who can grow further, even towards 'looking after' the welfare of the unemployed. The right kind of education and growth in responsibility can be two parts of a developing process, a saving process.

I have tried to show in this chapter how unnecessary unhappiness at work can be replaced by understanding and co-operation. I have shown the need for further education, for training. I have pointed out the need for management to learn more about the working of the human mind, for workers to learn more about the working of the economic system. I have suggested that really good training will not only lead to better relationships at work but to a knowledge of and interest in the community outside the factory walls, indeed even to a care for the workless. I believe that with good further education at work we could help to produce better balanced persons on both sides of industry, persons whose security enables them to look out in informed compassion towards the deprived. Indeed, as I was writing these last lines of this chapter, a young shop steward, the product of two really fine shop stewards' training courses, said to me on the telephone that what concerned him terribly was the worklessness of many of the young. He volunteered the statement. He was always a good skilled worker. Through first-rate, thought-provoking shop steward training, he has become a quietly confident, thoughtful, compassionate person.

NOTES

1   p. 92.
2   G. Sinclair: *I Only Work Here*, Holt, Rinehart and Winston, Sydney, 1979, p. 1.
3   ibid., pp. 24-72.
4   Routledge and Kegan Paul, 1977.
5   *Personnel Executive*, September 1981, pp. 19 and 21.
6   Frank Hay, in *World of Work*, Young Christian Workers, 1980, p. 3.
7   *Industrial and Commercial Training*, December 1981, pp. 407-9.
8   ibid., February 1981, p. 63.
9   ibid., December 1982, p. 398.
10 Jim Conway Foundation Week-end Seminar, 5 July 1981, pp. 16, 5, 4.
11 *The Professional Engineer*, June 1972, p. 30.
12 *Industrial and Commercial Training*, December 1981, pp. 404-13.
13 *Personnel Executive*, April 1982, p. 9.
14 *The First Circle*, Collins 1970, pp. 164, 15 (first published in English 1968).
15 *The Soviet Worker*, ed. L. Schapiro and J. Godson, Macmillan, 1981, p. 114.
16 ibid., pp. 234, 237, 238, 240, 241.
17 Jim Conway Memorial Foundation, 21-2 March 1982 Seminar Report, p. 7.
18 *Chrism, The St Raphael Quarterly*, November 1981, p. 10.
19 *The Human Condition*, University of Chicago Press, 1978, pp. 200-1 (first published 1958).

10

Unemployment under the Judgement of God

In this last chapter, I am trying to say that if the blight of unemployment is to be removed from millions of our fellow-citizens, it is possible that there may have to be sacrifices from many more millions of the employed. I hope to suggest ways of sacrifice. As we shall see, others in other countries suffering from unemployment have already looked at them. For Christians the concept of sacrifice, even of self-sacrifice, ought not to be altogether alien. For all persons of rationality and good will, experience teaches that sacrifice can and sometimes should be made in good causes. We grumble and pay up. I believe that many are anxious for all that is possible to be done, but do not know what to do. At a meeting which I addressed recently on the subject of unemployment, the chairman said: 'We all agree with every word which you have said. But what can we do about it?'

Lord Murray, formerly General Secretary of the Trades Union Congress, made in 1981 a controversial speech, the full import of which seemed scarcely at the time to be realized. He told union leaders that the unions must have a good look at themselves and at the image which they presented to the public. 'We have to show', he said, 'that we can balance our responsibilities to members with wider responsibilities.'[1] He is by no means the only union member capable of this kind of thinking. An engineer said to me recently, speaking from a humanist rather than from a Christian point of view, that men would have to learn to work with some ideals in mind, rather than with mere greed. He said that men worked better if they were less greedy and more balanced. I treasure in my mind the memory of both my electrician and my miner friends asserting that money was not and must not be the first aim. They said it and meant it. Selfishness is likely always to remain with us; but a time has come, with unemployment at its present height, for men of good will on both sides of industry (and elsewhere within the community) to consider seriously what they can do to prevent the ruination of the lives of many of the unemployed. Decent and kindly people at least ought to be able to see that prolonged mass unemployment is damaging to people. It is not good enough to blame 'the other side' for a situation which calls not so much for blame as for remedy. In a country such as Britain it is difficult to see how the unemployed can benefit unless the better off, in all sections of the community, are prepared to make sacrifices. I am assuming that there is unlikely to be a great increase in national prosperity in the near future.

I know of no more hard-headed and unsentimental a guide in industrial affairs than John Wellens, formerly of *Industrial and Commercial Training*. He writes that 'the socio-political situation for ever lags behind the technological one'. He reminds us of the technological revolution, the result of 'man's restless, questioning nature', which is taking place. He sees that there can be no turning back. There has, however, to be a turning forward to meet the social implications of the new technological changes. Mr Wellens points out that technological man has to be social man as well, has to realize not only his capacity for improving production but also his obligations to his fellow-men. Mr Wellens begs those who read him not to bemoan the malfunctions in the socio-political domain. 'The correct attitude', he declares, 'is to recognize the potential for conflict, anarchy and possibly collapse, and then to make such provisions as are required to forestall it.' Here surely is realism and constructiveness and reasonable optimism. In the 1985 Spring number of *Industrial and Commercial Training*, John Wellens writes that we must not 'become obsessed with the unemployment issue at the expense of all others'. He adds: 'A more reasonable attitude would be to focus on the central issue of building up a virile economy in harmony with today's and tomorrow's economic and social environment, so that relief of unemployment be a by-product of this rather than a primary aim.'

I have tried in chapter 8 to suggest some of the details of the building up of a virile economy. However, the fact remains that here and now young men and women (and many not so young) are rotting away because of unemployment. Something needs to be done now. We have to battle against unemployment now. When full employment has been restored, we have to ensure that nothing like it ever occurs again. Unemployment is a disease in the economic system. We have to see that it is eliminated, never mind by what rearrangement of work, knowing that we ourselves must somehow promote its elimination. Ordinary people ought to be able to see the need for this as clearly as they can see the need to repair flood or fire damage. We are not pleading for high idealism, but rather for that realism which causes our representatives in the House of Commons to vote for high income tax and those of us who pay it (grumblingly) to recognize that it is necessary if the nation itself and its people individually are to be secure and if those most in need are to be specially ministered to and cared for.

The man-in-the-street is not altogether thoughtless or uncaring. Yet he has for long been told that inflation is the prime enemy and deflation the aim. Consequently he is inclined to assent almost unconsciously to the supreme aim of overcoming inflation at almost any cost. He is not thoughtless about unemployment. He is depressed about the apparent hopelessness of curing it; and yet he knows that it is 'wrong'. We have to try to make the man-in-the-street see that it is morally wrong for him not to try to do something about it. We are, in fact, as a whole society under the judgement of God; for unemployed man is deprived of his right to be a working man and of his opportunity to develop as a human being. This is an unjust state of affairs. Man is robbed of what justice demands for him: the chance to satisfy and realize himself. It is a matter of justice; unemployment is unjust. This sense of the 'immorality' of unemployment has been expresssed by thoughtful politicians. It represents the guilty conscience of that section of the community which is prepared to think hard about the state of the unemployed. Edward Heath, in his impotence, cries out in Parliament against it, in agony as it were, and obviously not quite knowing what to do about it:

> I am not thinking about actions. I am thinking about the welfare of millions of people who are living miserable lives because they haven't got a job. There are those who are in their fifties who are being sacked and are saying, 'We shall never again in our lifetime have a job'.
>
> These are the people whom we have got to think about. How can we remain passive and do nothing? In these circumstances, I don't think we can. It will be a crime if we do.[2]

There is, on the other hand, a terrible tolerance of unemployment, a resigned willingness of the employed (and of many of the unemployed too) to accept it as a fact of life. People say, as we have heard, that with the development of technology, unemployment has come to stay and we must train the young for leisure rather than for work. They say these things brightly as if they had not been said before, as if they were original thoughts. Behind all this, there is the feeling, the knowledge that for us there is no real alternative society, no really satisfying alternative to work, that to be unemployed is to be deprived. All this hurts and ought to hurt. Consciences hurt because we are under the judgement of God. We, the workers, with our grass roots theology, our deep-buried inner consciousness of the will of God, know that it is not his will that great masses of our human brothers and sisters should have no work to do. We know that for society to tolerate unemployment is wrong. The system which permits it is under judgement, for it fails to render the justice which is due from man to man. The unemployed person himself feels under judgement. He is, in his own mind, an obvious failure. He has failed himself, has failed his family, by failing to get a job. He is depressed, humiliated, under financial stress. Inevitably, he comes to feel rejected by society, under the judgement of society. The society in turn in which he suffers unemployment is damaged, humiliated by his unemployed state.

I must insert here a special plea for a passionate consideration, combined with a hard-headed realism, for the state of the long-term unemployed. Those in the south of Britain may be ignorant of the extent of the problem and of the depth and grimness of its effect upon those who suffer from it. In a Herefordshire public house, on the border of Wales last week, I talked to a young labourer who was quite ignorant of what unemployment was like. 'We don't have it here,' he said. He was intelligent and willing to hear about it. As long ago as 1982, a Manpower Services paper on *Long-term Unemployment* declared that the long-term unemployed had less than a 30 percent chance of finding a job within twelve months. It added rather naïvely that 'employers appear not to want to hire people who have been out of work for long periods'. That is to under-state the reality. It referred to a Department of Employment survey showing that one-third of unemployed men and one-quarter of unemployed women exhaust all their savings during their unemployment. Thus it is to be retirement for them with no savings. Apart from those near to retirement the paper stated that unemployment was more prevalent among 18-24 year old people than for any other age group. It commented that 'the long-term psychological effect of unemployment on young people

. . . is likely to be more serious than for those in middle life'. The paper testified of all, old and young, that 'the vast majority want work and are actively looking for it'. Pathetically, it went on: 'Most of those who stop looking do so largely through ill-health. . .'[3] The danger now is that we are becoming used to all this. From my warm room in the midst of the intense cold of February 1985, I look out and see represatives of the homeless young unemployed passing by. I ask myself what I can do about it and am inclined to answer 'nothing'. This will not do. We must not accept implicitly the 'inevitable' decay of a majority of a large and seriously suffering element in the community. It was good, although an amelioration rather than a solution of the problem, to hear Sir Richard O'Brien advocating strongly that there should be a statutory obligation on employers to offer jobs when suitable to the long-term unemployed before offering them to others.

Unemployment is like a state of war. It is unnatural; it is unhappy; no one concerned can properly be at ease in it or with it. If there is the judgement of God upon the terrible, the dehumanizing state of the unemployed (but not, of course, upon the unemployed themselves), there is also the judgement of God upon the workers, the employed, upon all of us who in any way tolerate the continuance of unemployment. If and when our high wages or our working of over-time means that another person who could be given a job is not given one, we are especially under judgement. This is a hard saying. If it is too hard to take, let us at least accept beyond all quibbling the fact that our own development of full humanization must be impaired by the awful consciousness that our brother is deprived, is jobless. I have already, in chapter 5, quoted the great theologian Edward Schillebeeckx to this effect. Mine cannot be a full life, while my brother's and sister's are half-lives.

If we as a society are no longer to be under the judgement of God, we must begin to think decisively about what can be done to end mass unemployment. I have made in chapter 7 certain conventional suggestions for reflation without gross inflation. Yet most of those who support such a reflation only expect it to reduce unemployment, not to remove it. This is not good enough, not sufficiently just to our fellow-human beings. In view of the fact that the unemployed, in their weakness, can do very little for themselves, the responsibility for their readmission to working, self-respecting society, for their reconstitution towards the plenitude of humanity, must fall fairly and squarely upon the shoulders of the stronger, healthier, 'inner' members of society, the employed.

There will in fact, if I may dare to say so, have to be work-sharing, if the hard core of mass unemployment is to be eliminated. The most careful and thorough research into the possibilities of this needs to be done. Ordinary people might be willing to give up some hours at least of their jobs for others who have none. If people came to believe that reflation might reduce the number of the unemployed but would not cure unemployment, and that there was nothing but work-sharing which would give jobs to all the people who need them, people might be prepared to share their work with others. This would mean working shorter hours, perhaps shorter weeks. It would call for thoughtfulness, perhaps for unselfishness; but it would also have its rewards. People would grumble. Yet if they could see unemployment being cured, they might submit with bad grace (as they submit to high taxation). They would be aware that the almost incredibly great needs of others were at last being met. 'All for one, one for all'. Thoughtfulness for others is painful but not impossible. 'The only life worth living', says the socialist Lord Soper to socialists, 'is the caring life'.[4] People are able and often willing to care, if they are shown clearly what there is to care about and exactly how to set about caring. At least until this time of writing, there has been scarcely any appeal for people to give up jobs or part of their jobs for those out of work; there has been no appeal to people even to think about these things. Overtime has continued to be done, and (if I may so so) over-done, despite official trade union opposition to it. Of course, it pays employers to encourage over-time. They have less insurance to pay.

What does already exist is the demand for the shorter working week: the thirty-nine hour week that already exists in many cases, the thirty-five hour week hoped for. People outside industry have little sympathy for these reductions of working hours, because they do not know how hard and steadily many people work and how tired they tend to become. People who have read in the papers of some British Leyland night worker asleep on his shift neither check on the accuracy of the report nor as to whether this kind of thing is typical. They condemn the work-shy without bothering to discover how rare (or how common) the problem of work-shyness is. In fact, the ordinary worker is not work-shy. Again and again, in factory after factory, I have asked myself how workers, male and female, manage to maintain the pace, the effort. The answer is that many of them do it at the cost of extreme fatigue. One of the much-maligned A.S.L.E.F. train drivers, in the course of his fight to maintain his eight hour day, explained what it meant for him: 'An eight hour day may mean six hours of driving. And that is about enough.' Considering the inevitable responsibility of driving a train under modern U.K. conditions, what he says does not sound unreasonable. Indeed it ought not to be considered unreasonable. Many tired workers doze in their chairs when they come home and have little to contribute to family life, to the maintenance of their marriages, to the up-bringing of growing children. Week-ends often do not bring the refreshment which is needed, because the worker is too tired to profit from a short week-end. When Eddie takes his children to the cinema in Liverpool, he always goes off to sleep. All this fatigue is worsened in almost every way by the fact that many workers who can get over-time take it. The extra earnings from over-time frequently make all the difference between discomfort and comfort on the worker's wage. 'It pays the tax,' says an Oxford bus-driver. It also exhausts the driver. Quite apart from work-sharing, there is a real case for the shorter day and the shorter working week, with week-ends that will not only repair the damage done by fatigue but which will reinvigorate.

As I am in the course of writing this page, I take part in a programme for television with some school children. In the course of answering the inevitable question as to what I should do about unemployment, I explain briefly the concept of work-sharing. The children remain apathetic, for they do not realize the need. What amazed me was the reaction of the adults. One after another, they came up to me, mature, highly competent television and teaching staff, to tell me that as I had talked to the youngsters, they had caught the vision of work-sharing: of the shorter day, of the shorter week. Just for a moment indeed each one of them had seen what life could be like, if you had time and if you were not too tired to enjoy it.

There is, however, the obvious question of finance. There is the massive problem of the financing of any considerable work-sharing scheme, where many more people would be employed, and where nearly all would work for a shorter time. If such a scheme were to make a substantial impact on the present unemployment figures, the mind boggles at the prospect of adequate remuneration for all concerned. There have, however, already been some attempts to begin to grapple with the problem. Paul Blyton and Stephan Hill, writing in the *National Westminster Bank Quarterly Review* for November 1981, quoted interesting figures. These are to the effect that the government could pay an unemployed person up to 90 percent of the average manual wage for his work and still make a saving on its budget deficit. We shall return to the cost of financing an equitable scheme of work-sharing later in the chapter. Messrs Blyton and Hill told us that this large government payment which would in fact involve a net saving for it would take account of the welfare benefits paid to the unemployed person and also the revenue from taxes and national insurance which that person would pay when employed. They wrote: 'The high costs of unemployment are well documented. Most immediate are the transfer costs from the taxpayer in the form of welfare payments (redundancy pay, unemployment benefit, family income and other supplements) . . . More difficult but no less significant are the social costs of unemployment manifested in depressed areas and increasing social disorder.' How much did Toxteth cost, how much Railton Road? How much would be saved if there were no more Toxteths and Brixtons? Let us never forget the terrible cost to the Exchequer of the miners' dispute of 1984-5.

The same authors go on to plead with the trade unions to take the benefits of increased productivity as a result of technology in the form of a reduced working week rather than in that of increased wages. This would provide an opportunity for increasing employment to meet any growth in demand.[5] We are by various routes in our search for a cure for unemployment at least catching a glimpse of a hard fact. If there is a radical redistribution of available work, there may have to be in certain cases (but not in all) an end to annual wage increases. If workers are to learn to care more for the state of their unemployed brothers and sisters, they will have to learn also to appreciate and face the cost of translating such care into action. Constructive good will towards the unemployed will have to be translated into the acceptance of an incomes policy of some sort.

I am trying to challenge, to provoke to hard thought, rather than to develop a detailed plan. While the awful thought of the financing of shorter hours and shared work is sinking down, let us turn to the more cheerful subject of the advantages of shorter hours for present workers. Under work-sharing, those now unemployed would enter into industry where they would not exchange the misery of unemployment for the fatigue of unnecessarily long hours of work. At the 1979 Labour Party Conference, Lord Gormley, then Mr Joe Gormley, President of the National Union of Mineworkers, supported a resolution on the question of unemployment and the shorter working week. He spoke of the shorter working week as a contributing factor to the reduction of unemployment:

> I am not going to suggest that to achieve these objectives we are going to sit back and say it must be the Government's responsibility. I think we in the trade union movement have a responsibility too. We cannot sit back . . . and allow the unemployment figures to rise in the whole of Europe, and Britain in particular. We cannot sit back and say that, because we are all right, it does not matter. It does matter, when half the people in Britain who could be producing wealth are unable to produce wealth because they are unemployed.
>
> Many of us have taken steps to try to deal with this question. . . . At the moment a man of 60 with 20 years' underground service can retire this year on between 85-90 percent of his take-home pay until he is 65, index-linked. We believe this will create a better atmosphere in the lower age level within the pits. We have done it without the need to go to the Government to ask for their support. We decided it had to be. . . . We have to tell people they have the right not to work all the time. They are entitled to enjoy life as well. And that is the way we look at things in the mining industry. We are not born to work; we are born to enjoy life. And work is part of it. But it is not the only part of it. It is part of a philosophy of life, and if we could create all the wealth we need for the welfare state, for education, for better roads, for better hospitals, by everybody working one or two days out of seven, what is wrong with it? I hope that in this trade union movement and in this Labour movement we can get this idea in our minds. We have got to tackle the problem today, because, with the micro-chip industry that is coming upon us, it will become more and more

urgent, and unless we start today we will be just in the middle of a holocaust in 10 years' time from now. . . . If all the people in Britain were working and producing wealth . . . if they were only working one or two days a week . . . what the hell is wrong with that? What is wrong with that philosophy?

The speech was applauded; yet it seemed at the time not to have been taken to heart or its reasoning seriously followed up.

However, in this country and overseas various persons and bodies have been thinking and speaking (less bluntly) on similar lines. The T.U.C. reported as early as August 1981 that already more than half the country's manual workers have a standard working week of under forty hours. A sweet manufacturer has proposed a cut from forty to thirty-seven hours, coupled with a four day week.[6] Earlier still, in 1980, the Institute of Manpower Studies looked hard at the E.E.C. Social Affairs Directorate's proposals concerning a return to full employment. These concluded that 'work-sharing could also aid progress towards newer patterns of work'. However, the proposals noted that one in three British workers worked an average of 6.3 hours' overtime each week. The I.M.S., echoing E.E.C. proposals, thought that there was at that time 'very little awareness at the local level of any need for work-sharing and no real sympathy with the concept'.[7] That makes sad reading. As a B.B.C. news-reader on 24th August 1982 commented with reference to the highest unemployment figures at that time ever recorded in Great Britain: 'The country seems to be getting used to high unemployment figures'.

However remote we may seem at present from constructive work-sharing, part-time work does continue to grow in Britain. So does job-sharing. In a bank, for example, one girl may work one week and another alternate weeks with her. The concept of sharing has at least been born. In France in 1982, an Enabling Act reduced the statutory working week from 40 to 39 hours, extended annual paid leave to five weeks, and offered State aid for working time cuts in industry. It was a start.

In the House of Commons and House of Lords, junior Ministers at various times in answers to questions have revealed no willingness on the part of the Department of Employment to consider work-sharing seriously. It is assumed that work-sharing would necessarily increase costs and make British products less competitive. I have attempted in this chapter to suggest ways in which this increase of cost could be avoided. A letter from the Ministry to myself (from which I am permitted to quote) refers to work-sharing as a 'manipulating' of hours and patterns of work. Indeed, a respected Non-stipendiary Ministry engineer friend of mine writes to me to say how difficult it would be to alter 'traditional patterns of work'. We are up, however, against an altogether untraditional level of unemployment. Nevertheless, some breaches in the tradition have been affected. There is a 38-hour week in the chemical industry, a 37-hour week for Mobil, Shell and Conoco in the oil sector, a 35-hour week for Metal Box in South London. The Westland Group, incorporating Westland Helicopters and British Hovercraft, introduced a basic 32.5-hour week in 1984, in return for a double day shift for technicians employed on computer-aided design equipment. From the union side this was hailed as a 'land-mark in British Trade unionism . . . a model of its kind that others will be seeking to emulate'. There was even a Temporary Short-Time Working Compensation Scheme introduced in 1979, and a Job Splitting Scheme in 1983. However, neither scheme was promoted or received with enthusiasm. It is also of interest that the West Germans and Belgians both have legal limits to the amount of overtime that is permitted to be worked. It is significant that as long ago as 1978 a study made by the European Commission showed that 51 percent of the total working population in the Community would prefer shorter hours for the same pay as against 42 percent in favour of better pay for the same hours. John Cahill, policy adviser on employment to the C.B.I., has actually implied (in 1984) that work-sharing would be acceptable if workers would at least forego part of a pay rise in return for more leisure.[8] Minds move slowly.

Slow movement, while the unemployed suffer on, is not good enough. In a prolonged period of national crisis such as this, there has to be hard thought on the part of all capable of rationality, and leadership capable of intelligible appeal within democracy. There has to come, from political and social and religious thinkers prepared to give that sorely needed lead, challenge both to self-interest and to unselfishness. It is in the self-interest of all that our fellow-citizens at present unemployed should find work, lest in their unemployment and inevitable consequent dehumanization they not only suffer themselves but cause all society to suffer.

None of us have enjoyed Toxteth and Brixton. The prospect of more Toxteths and Brixtons as unemployment goes on ought to make us very concerned (and anxious to remove the root cause of such troubles). There needs to be an appeal to unselfishness, one of those appeals which can be only rarely made because of the human resistance to them. Such appeals were made and succeeded to a considerable extent in the two world wars. Many men and women offered their lives, their service, their money; they endured legislation which limited their freedom and their style of living. All this was for a cause. Sacrifice was asked for, and sacrifice was offered. We need now to persuade people that the cause of removing the scourge of unemployment is a good cause and one worthy of sacrifice. I am arguing for a drastic and radical manner of dealing with the cancer of mass unemployment. I am asking all sorts of people, trade unionists, employers, Members of Parliament, Christians, to consider very seriously whether worksharing on a big scale may not be far better for society as a whole than a system which is seemingly resigned to mass unemployment for years to come. I am asking for thorough research, for education for both sides of industry, for painstaking thought for all who have any sort of social conscience within the community. At the risk of continuing repetitivity, I admit that there will have to be some losses in wages. There will be gains in time for recreation, gains in health, and gains for the Exchequer in the reduction of the costs of unemployment. Out of these (as we have seen) there can be subsidies to wages or even a basic subsistence allowance. In all my appeal for willingness to sacrifice, to suffer some reduction in wages, I am bearing in mind the need to hold down costs of production and to avoid inflation. There must be, for the sake of the workless at least, a new prices and incomes policy. Few will care for it; but many could come to see the point of it, if it were part of an intelligible plan to cure unemployment. In the end, it will be taken for granted as an element in a just society intolerant of unemployment.

Here and there in Britain, the idea is being received. On television, a young Preston electrician says, 'If they could cut the working week down to give some-one else a job, that would be better'. The speaker was a rough-speaking lad. It was good to hear him. At least some are beginning to think. Dr Paul Blyton, a lecturer in Industrial Relations at the Institute of Science &

Technology of the University of Wales, writes again: 'The time seems ripe for a more serious examination of work-sharing and of the potential benefits not only for government and unions but also for employers'. In his *National Westminster Bank Quarterly Review* article (with Stephan Hill), he has pleaded for work-sharing to be taken seriously, to be carefully prepared for, and the idea of it fostered at the individual places where the practicalities could be worked out. He pointed out that in six E.E.C. countries over half the working populations, when offered the choice between more pay and shorter hours, chose the latter. This bears out my own researches amongst miners and electricians. He claims that, with a small amount of government assistance, 'employers could gain substantially from introducing one or other of the work-sharing schemes'.[9]

Bryan Bartlett, a lecturer at the S.W. Regional Management Centre, Bristol, comes out strongly for a radical new approach to work-sharing. He believes that a shorter working week could be so structured as to allow for a 'pool of trained workers' who could fill the gaps. He writes that 'there is little doubt that a radical re-thinking of the working week will be both necessary and inevitable'.[10] At any rate, there ought to be among leaders who help to shape public opinion a new interest in new work patterns. In West Germany, for example, the unemployed are encouraged to take part-time jobs. In Australia there is much encouragement for job-sharing, where two people are voluntarily sharing the responsibility of one job. This gives to each person the satisfaction of being at work, of doing a job, an identity status. I have suggested already how the financing of the process might be arranged. The Equal Opportunities Commission published a booklet on part-time work called *Job-sharing*. It highlights areas which should be covered in job-sharing agreements: pay, sick pay, overtime, maternity/paternity arrangements, pensions, training, promotion. It states that job-sharing in the United Kingdom is largely restricted to the public or semi-public sector. Many people in Britain have no idea that such a work pattern is possible. We have scarcely begun as a nation to think along these lines.

Yet there are faint signals of an awakening to great need and towards its solution. It has dawned on some of the employed that they can help the unemployed. Steel workers at Ebbw Vale in

September 1981 refused to do any more over-time while there were unemployed steel workers available. Mr Bill Sirs and their Union supported them. In February 1983, 500 workers at a fork lift factory in Scotland accepted a 13 percent pay cut. This was in return for a promise from the American President of the company that a £40 million expansion programme would take place and that this would create 1,000 new jobs over the next few years.

At a July 1981 seminar of the Jim Conway Memorial Foundation of trade unionists, the Senior Lecturer in Industrial Relations from the Thames Polytechnic made a strong plea to the trade union movement. After mentioning that 54 percent of British workers worked 10.3 hours of over-time each week, he asked trade unionists to consider how they could directly help the unemployed not only by reducing over-time but also by work-sharing. The quiet reply by one worker to the effect that work-sharing means wage-sharing needs to be frankly faced and seriously researched. Blyton and Hill in the *National Westminster Review* concluded that 'with mounting pressure on the government to introduce more measures to alleviate unemployment, subsidizing work-sharing schemes could represent a valuable aspect of a broader employment programme.'

Mr John Wellens, as usual, is definitive and drastically logical in his demands on industry. He writes that all the 'know-how' is available, the workers with the technical skills, competent management, redundant plants, closing shipyards, 'idle workers at all levels languishing on the dole'. We pay out, he says, huge sums to pay them for not working; all the ingredients are there, he writes, just lying around unused. He quotes from a parliamentary answer in 1981 that an unemployed single man then cost the country £4,835 per annum, and an unemployed married man with two children £6,006. He calls this 'a system in a state of collapse' 'a vale of tears' with 'all the bits lying around'.[11] He believes that 'we will have to take some positive action' for the situation to come right, 'some attempt to manage change', some constructive policy, some control.[12]

My personal belief is that if we are to cure unemployment we shall have to come to a much shorter working day (with two shifts) or to the three or four day working week. I prefer the former. If serious social discontent develops, as mass unemployment continues and even grows, it may need to be more urgently and more seriously considered. John Hawkwood on the centre page of *The Guardian* suggested years ago an acceptable form of work-sharing.[13] In his wisdom he writes to me that work-sharing is 'so obviously the only possible way that the unemployment situation can be improved'. He adds that 'the approach everyone seems to take, i.e. job creation, is so obviously a non-starter'. He suggests that we must cease to cling to our traditional concept of the 40 hour (or 30 hour) week. On the assumption that one in ten of the work force is out of work, let each employed person give up one-tenth of his work, so as to give work to the unemployed. He agrees that this is 'a sweeping over-simplification'. He also suggests the giving up by those who wish to do so of one day's work a week. He believes that this might be acceptable 'if they felt they would lose less than a day's pay'. He is trying to make people realize that 'something less than a full-time job is feasible, practicable and desirable'. He adds, 'An old-fashioned full-time job is rather anti-social, a luxury reserved for those who can afford it'. In answer to the claim that there would be inevitable opposition from the unions (because of reduced pay for reduced work), he suggests tax concessions for those prepared to reduce their hours of work, and a very slight increase in the tax paid by full-time workers. He envisages a further reduction of the National Insurance contribution paid by employers for workers on reduced time, in order to encourage them to employ the unemployed. All this, he writes to me, should be 'entirely voluntary on the part of the workers'. The tax concessions for those prepared to work the shorter week would be covered by the reduced cost to the nation of having fewer on the dole. John Hawkwood's suggestions deserve the consideration which (so far as I know) they have not yet received. He goes on to say to me: 'I would go so far as to suggest that people who opt for a shorter working week could actually be eligible for a basic subsistence allowance as a further incentive.' He believes strongly that people should be rewarded for working the shorter week and making room for the unemployed.

If these ideas seem too drastic or impracticable, they are at least challenges to all who are prepared to think about the state of the unemployed (and not merely to regret it). There are ordinary people who are already beginning to think along these lines. Even the Conservative Minister in charge of information technology declared to the British Association in 1982 that 'in less than twenty years' time most of us will be working a four-day week, forty weeks a year'.[14] Perhaps the process of achieving something like this might, in the interest of the unemployed, be speeded up. Our electrician from Preston affirms that 'if they could cut the working week down to give someone else a job, that would be better'. That there has to be a revolution in attitudes to work is one of the themes of Clive Jenkins' and Barrie Sherman's micro-technology-welcoming and thought-provoking *Collapse of Work*.[15] Indeed there must be such a revolution if the unemployed are to be rescued and society saved. 'Most people won't get involved,' said a friend to me earlier today. It is not necessary for 'most people to get involved'. It is only necessary for a keen leading minority to become very seriously involved. Let all who really care about the future of work in Britain become involved, help to bring about a revolution in thinking among those who think at all. Let everyone who cares about the human future of the unemployed do his little bit in such a cause. On television again, Sir Hector Laing, the industrialist, pleads for retirement at fifty-five for the workers, in order to make room at work for the young unemployed. Better indeed to be unemployed at fifty-five than at eighteen. However, let us remember that having nothing to do is no joy to anyone at any age, and early retirement is not a satisfactory or a satisfying solution for the early retired (except for those wearied and aged beyond their years, and for the relatively few with consuming hobbies, active cultural pursuits or organized voluntary work).

Sir Hector is rightly concerned about the state of the unemployed. On the same programme he says, 'If they don't get work, they will lose the urge to work'. Indeed, he is right. Unemployment is tiring, debilitating. What many of the unemployed will not lose for some time is that 'urge to change the environment' which we considered in Chapter 1. Many of them will become vandals and rioters on occasions. They, being human, must leave their mark upon something, being deprived of the opportunity to leave their mark proudly on the making of a Daimler or of an engine for Zambia. An experienced friend of mine is just back from business in the poorer parts of Sheffield, Manchester, Liverpool. In all three places he found large numbers of youths hanging about on the streets all day, waiting for something to happen. Of course, nothing happened. However, some day it might; and they wuld be ready for it, for anything. We, the employed, may have become used to their unemployment. To us it may have become in course of time acceptable. That ought not to be. To the unemployed, at least until their humanity has been irreparably damaged, it is and must be intolerable, unacceptable. It ought to be so for us.

We, the British, amongst all political parties, remain strangely oblivious (or ignorant) concerning movements of thought in other industrial countries in the European Economic Community. It was calculated at the end of 1984 that there are 12.75 million workers currently seeking work in E.E.C. countries. The O.E.C.D. calculates that 20 million new jobs will be needed in the industrialized world to stop unemployment from rising over the next five years. In Europe the trade unions are in the forefront of the demand to make work-sharing the alternative to growing mass unemployment. The President of the European Trades Union Confederation (E.T.U.C.) has declared that 'there is no viable solution to unemployment today other than the sharing out of the amount of work to be done among more people, thanks to a cut in working hours'. Much research has been done in Europe relating to the possibilities and limitations of work-sharing as an instrument of employment policy. As early as 1981, the European Parliament debated and resolved in favour of a report on the adaptation of working time drawn up by its Committee on Social Affairs and Employment. The policy was eventually included in a Council of Ministers resolution on Community action to combat unemployment. A small 'Job-Splitting Scheme' exists in Britain.

Despite its not over-large congregations, the Church might help a little. Indeed it might even now be possible for bishops and archbishops on great occasions, when Members of Parliament and leaders of the community are gathered before them, to speak of the world rather than of the Church. They might even speak out and challenge on behalf of the unemployed. A prophetic appeal might be made for justice for 'the weakest, the poorest and the most deprived sections of the community' (to quote our Adviser to the House of Lords Select Committee on Unemployment). It seems that prophets are needed to stir nations. In university chaplaincies, in college chapels, in parish and other churches throughout towns and countryside, week by week, men and

145

women of God, clerical and lay, have an opportunity to speak to a fairly thoughtful, quite considerable minority of the nation. Would it not be possible, in God's name, to say constructively and without giving offence, that it is immoral to stand by and to do nothing about mass unemployment except to wait for 'better times' or to provide alternative 'cultural' pursuits for passing the time? We must try to avoid bitterness, but not pity combined with hard thinking. Christianity is all about costly and loving service. This must surely appeal to many who call themselves Christians but are not churchgoers. To them, as well as to churchgoers, it must become obvious that in their present state our duty to the unemployed demands the maximum of hard thought and dedicated activity. There must be many who, once they realized the need, would respond. There is seeing, there is judging and there must be action (say the Young Christian Workers).

War has often been described as 'evil', despite the innocence of many of those who take part in it. Archbishop Davidson in 1914 called it 'devil's work'. Certainly no less evil is unemployment; it is an evil which has been allowed to grow because thoughtlessly we did not realize its gravity. We have tolerated what is intolerable. Because it is evil, it ought to provoke all of good will to hard thought and strong action. In this dehumanizing evil of unemployment, the interest of the United Kingdom and that of the kingdom of God coincide. For the community's sake, for the individual's sake, and for God's sake, mass unemployment must be eliminated. Because it is evil, God must surely be concerned, and he will truly be served by the curing of it. Society has made of the unemployed person an alien in our midst: mentally sick, with a tendency towards isolating himself, weak and voiceless. The Christian must approach this social problem with reason informed by faith. That faith ought to render him passionate and determined.

Let us consider what is meant by the kingdom of God and how relevant to mass unemployment the concept of it may be. Jesus preached the kingdom of God by the shores of Galilee. He tried by his parables to make it a regulative principle for his followers' lives. He did not invent the concept of the kingdom of God. He found it alive when he began his ministry, preserved as it was in the history, psalmody and prophecy of the Old Testament. J. Moltmann tell us that the scarlet thread which runs through the

Bible is the continuing history of the kingdom of God.[16] God had spoken to Samuel saying that 'Israel would not have him to be their king'. (*1 Samuel* 8,7). Yet their king he truly was. The Psalmist proclaims him: 'The Lord is king; he is clothed in majesty.' (*Psalm* 97,1 and 9), This 'Lord of Hosts', sings the Psalmist, is indeed 'my King and my God'. (84,3). 'With these eyes,' says Isaiah the prophet, 'I have seen the King, the Lord of Hosts.' (6,5). Jesus inherited this tradition of God's kingship, sang the Psalms which proclaimed it. So he preached it, developing the concept into the central doctrine of his gospel. 'Jesus came into Galilee proclaiming the Gospel of God: "The time has come; the kingdom of God is upon you".' (*S. Mark* 1,15). 'The usual object of the preaching of Jesus', says the Jesuit, J. Bonsirven, 'was the Reign of God.'[17] When Jesus proclaimed God's kingdom, people understood that he meant that they were to enter, as it were, of their own free will into the realm of God, to enter God's service, to become obedient to his will. St Paul wrote that 'the kingdom of God is not a matter of talk, but of power', and that it is 'not eating and drinking, but justice, peace, and joy'. (*I Corinthians* 4,20 and *Romans* 14,17).

There might be a new respect for the Church if it were to preach this and to spell out what is implied by 'justice'. The image of God as king might well become comprehensible to people for whom at present the concept of anyone's powerful kingship seems old-fashioned, out of date. In the quiet of their own souls many people outside the Church acknowledge and respect God. I can think of many workers who have genuine respect for what is right and to whom the concept of 'God's will in God's kingdom' might be made meaningful. Jesus said very strongly, 'I must give the news of the kingdom of God . . . for that is what I was sent to do'. (*S. Luke* 4,43). He sent out his disciples to say, 'The kingdom of God has come close to you'. (*S. Luke* 10,9). To the would-be disciple who wanted time to bury his father before following him, he said, 'You must go and announce the kingdom of God'. (*S. Luke* 9,60). K. L. R. Otto described the conception of the kingdom of God as a 'dynamic' one, as the advent of 'an inbreaking realm'.[18] It was not a concept intended by Jesus to be neglected by Christians.

Bishop John Taylor (formerly of Winchester) writes that the kingdom is 'not yet', that 'it does not lie within the span of world history,' that 'it belongs to another dimension'.[19] Yet he agrees that Jesus's task was 'actually to inaugurate it', that 'the kingdom arrives from beyond'. He says that we are called to live 'the life style of the kingdom', that it has to be lived 'in anticipation of its arrival'. I would say that the kingdom of God is already firmly planted in our midst and that it is God's intention that it should grow on earth. In any case we agree that the concept of the kingdom of God challenges us to attempt here and now to live according to God's will. The will of God indeed ought to be authoritative for Christians. It is a concept which could be made meaningful and challenging to many within the community. Bishop Taylor says that there is within the Church 'a quality of fellowship that will send its members triumphantly into the fight against the machine-like institutions.'[20] If what he says is true, the Church and others in sympathy with Christian beliefs and aims ought to begin to think and to say what is implied for today in the conception of the kingdom of God and in that of the will of God for man. Let the trumpets sound, especially if a determination that the kingdom shall come (as we say in the *Lord's Prayer*) means also a determination that unemployment shall end.

In so far as we believe that work, creative activity towards a social end, work that changes the environment and humanizes the person, is God's will for man, we can see that unemployment has no role in his kingdom. We know that it is God's will for his unemployed people that they should find work and have a chance to start to fulfil themselves.

Once Christians (and others) start to think and speak like that, they are into politics, 'the science and art of government'. For the kingdom's sake, let us go in open-eyed, and prepared to ally ourselves with all others of good will intent upon justice and the restoration of the welfare of the weak and needy. Long ago the Lord of the Church echoed a great Hebrew prophet:

> He has sent me to announce good news to the poor, to proclaim release for prisoners and recovery of sight for the blind; to let the broken victims go free.
>
> (*S. Luke* 4, 18; cp. *Isaiah* 61,1)

With other men of good will, Christians must enunciate principles at least, perhaps details too, as to what should be done for the unemployed. There is need for the broken victims to go free. It has been said many times that the problem of unemployment will not just go away. It ought not to be allowed to fester indefinitely. The Bishop of Hereford speaks for all who take the gospel of the kingdom seriously:

> We've got to be political, and by that I don't mean we've got to be allied with a political party. But it's absolutely essential that the Church now speaks. We've gone on doing good work, hospital work really, helping those who are at the mercy of those in power. Now we've got to be prophetic to the power-holders and the decision-makers. . . .
>
> Once you get into that area, you are bound to be political. You needn't be party-minded, . . . but I think that in your thinking about the future and what might happen, that the way we're being pressured by events from outside is from the Lord; I think the Lord is pressuring us to be prophetic. You can be prophetic as a community, as well as the individual working on the fringes of deprived areas and where there are real tensions, racial or otherwise. Justice is going to be the big debate in the Church. And justice is political.[21]

The prosperous and many of the employed are so isolated in the privacy of their homes from the unemployed in their distress that only some sort of clarion call, some 'prophecy', some 'word of God', can rouse them. In so far as we do nothing, we are under the judgement of God. Let there be no mistake about that. Let us then get involved as best we can in politics 'for the kingdom's sake' and let us try to involve others in the politics of the kingdom of God. Let me add a quotation from Bishop David Jenkins, of the William Temple Foundation:

> Those of us who can should use whatever opportunities and influence we have to persuade the Church at large to give up its stupid and faithless fear of political commitment and involvement. Since politics so shape human beings, those who believe that Jesus is Lord must be concerned with them. Since God, as He is in Jesus, is involved in the concrete and the immediate we must be prepared for the inevitable involvement in compromise, uncertainty, wrongness and partiality which is inseparable from practical politics and practical action. It is God who again and again will correct us, not faithless attempts to stay out of it all.[22]

I do not choose to conclude with a reference to the kingdom of God and to the Christian's duty to involve himself in politics. I am aware of how few take that kingdom or that duty seriously. However, I am also aware of how considerable a minority there is in Britain of concerned and caring people. We all know that it is minorities which get things done. It is in the education and development and influence of such a minority that hope for the future lies. A considerable minority may grow into a concern for the unemployed based upon some knowledge of them. To know them is in some measure to suffer with them. The American Jesuit, Richard McCormick, says that this knowledge (which is fellow-suffering) is becoming more necessary. 'What is so lacking', he says, 'in contemporary life is passion.' He goes on to say:

> Passion is the beginning of any true moral responsibility – It is the inner identification with the suffering and the downtrodden. It is that personal start-up that gets us off-centre a bit – and propels us to examine our consciences, comforts, and priorities. To develop genuine passion and concern, I believe we have to be exposed to those who suffer.[23]

Let us who read and think try so to expose ourselves. Then let us see what we can do about it. In the meantime, whether or not we recognize God's kingdom, we are certainly under the judgement of God.

NOTES

1 *The Guardian*, 4 February 1981, p. 1.
2 *The Guardian*, 16 March 1982, p. 5.
3 M.S.C. *Long Term Unemployment*, 1982, pp. 7, 36, 12, 38, 37, 45, 8.
4 D. Soper: *Socialism*, Christian Socialist Movement, 1980, p.15.
5 pp. 37, 43.
6 *The Guardian*, 31 August 1981, p. 16.
7 *Manpower Studies*, August 1980, pp. 14-15.
8 *National Westminster Bank Quarterly Review*, February 1985, pp. 30-37.
9 ibid., November 1981.
10 *Personal Executive*, October 1982, pp. 36-8.
11 *Industrial and Commercial Training*, March 1981, p. 83.
12 ibid., August 1981, p. 271.
13 8 September 1982, p. 13.
14 *The Guardian*, 9 September 1982, p. 12.
15 Eyre Methuen, 1979.

16 *The Trinity and the Kingdom of God (op.cit.)*, p. 95.
17 *Le Règne de Dieu*, Aubier, Paris, 1956, p. 7.
18 *The Kingdom of God and the Son of Man*, Lutterworth, 1943, p. 545.
19 *Your Kingdom Come*, World Council of Churches, Geneva, 1980, p. 133.
20 ibid., pp. 133-4.
21 *The Franciscan*, September 1981, pp. 131, 133.
22 *Ministry in the Town Hall*, William Temple Foundation, 1982, p. 35.
23 *How Brave a New World? (op.cit.)*, p. 45.